TEACHING MATHEMATICS
IN THE PRIMARY SCHOOL

Teaching Mathematics in the Primary School

Gill Bottle

and the primary mathematics team at
Canterbury Christ Church University College

continuum

Continuum

The Tower Building
11 York Road
London SE1 7NX

80 Maiden Lane
Suite 704
New York, NY 10038

www.continuumbooks.com

First published 2005
Reprinted 2006, 2007 (twice)

© Gill Bottle 2005

British Library Cataloguing-in-Publication Data
A catalogue record for this book is available from the British Library.

ISBN   978–0–8264-7258-8 hardback)
        978–0–8264-7259-5 (paperback)

Designed and typeset by Ben Cracknell Studios
Printed and bound in Great Britain by MPG Books Ltd, Bodmin, Cornwall

Contents

Preface

Teaching Mathematics in the Primary School has been written as a collaborative project by members of the Primary Mathematics team at Canterbury Christ Church University College. Those members are Gill Bottle, Donna Birrell, Gina Donaldson, Andrew Harris, Cathy Lawrence, Helen Taylor and Jon Wild.

The Canterbury Primary Mathematics team is well respected nationally and has achieved grade one in its last three Ofsted inspection reports. The team felt that readers would benefit from a book drawing on their wide-ranging expertise, breadth of knowledge, collective skills and extensive school experience.

Writing this book has been important to the Primary Mathematics team at Canterbury because we feel that too many training opportunities focus only on the delivery of the National Numeracy Strategy (DfEE, 1999) or concentrate on the development of personal mathematics understanding. This book, therefore, focuses on current theory in practical contexts that are directly applicable to the classroom and on the teaching of mathematics as a discipline in its own right.

Introduction

This book examines the development of children's mathematical learning and how current research can help practitioners to underpin the development of children's mathematical understanding. It therefore has potential both as a textbook for teacher training students on 3–11 courses and as a reference book for newly qualified teachers and teachers who want to integrate methods related to current research into their teaching. It explores the learning and teaching of mathematics in settings for children between the ages of 3 and 11.

There are many books that examine different subject areas within mathematics and look at the subject knowledge required to teach those areas. This book is different in that it looks at key issues in current research and how these issues may be addressed on a practical level. It considers the connections between teaching, managing, planning and assessment and presents ideas about how practitioners might enhance children's mathematical understanding and ability to use mathematics in a variety of contexts.

Chapter 1 looks at mathematics as a subject area. We examine current perceptions of the nature of mathematics and what is known about ways of facilitating mathematical understanding in children aged between 3 and 11. In the past mathematics was viewed as a set of procedures and principles. More recently, however, the idea that mathematics is socially situated and bound up in and inseparable from real life has been developed. This chapter sets out to explain current thinking and looks at how current perceptions of the nature of mathematics have manifested in practice.

Chapter 2 builds on chapter 1 by focusing on children's understanding of mathematics. We examine general principles of teaching and learning in relation to the theory and discuss the importance of contextualizing mathematics to enhance understanding of the relationships between mathematical areas and mathematics and real life. This includes looking at ideas from other countries, particularly Dutch ideas. Children using and applying their mathematics is a major focus and the chapter includes the use of investigations, games, problem-solving, stories as starting points and cross-curricular ideas.

Effective teaching can enhance mathematics learning and chapter 3 uses classroom examples to exemplify points that are made about important aspects of teaching. We explore the importance of effective interaction between the children and the teacher and with the learning materials presented and of making connections across different aspects of mathematics and between symbols, images, words and diagrams. This chapter also looks at the importance of effective questioning and at the use of mathematical modelling. Finally it reviews the ways in which ICT can be used in practical, everyday contexts within the classroom.

The aim of chapter 4 is to outline the different ways in which resources may be used by both teachers and pupils in mathematics lessons. We explore the suitability of resources and illustrates this by using practical classroom examples including the use of the everyday environment (natural and man-made), everyday artefacts, role-play equipment, stories, games, displays, other adults, ICT and published resources. The broad range of resources available for use in the mathematics classroom, the advantages of using them and the potential dangers about which teachers need to be aware are examined and the differences between structured and unstructured apparatus and their respective uses are considered. We discuss issues about effective practice in relation to the use of resources, such as the selection and evaluation of resources, the influence of resources upon assessment outcomes and the ways in which resources might allow, inhibit or address the formation of misconception.

Chapter 5 discusses how to organize and manage mathematics lessons, concentrating not only on the organizational aspects but also on how best to fully engage the children. As pupil participation is key to successful mathematics teaching and learning, possible solutions and strategies are highlighted. Promoting an environment where children are keen to participate is an essential tool that class teachers should master. As well as this, mathematics can be best learnt where a variety of learning strategies are encouraged. Children can work as individuals, in pairs or as part of small groups. Whatever the arrangement, this chapter seeks to identify the wealth of opportunities available with pupil groupings, and attempts to analyse when such groupings are most appropriate.

Chapter 6 looks at the assessment and planning cycle with particular reference to mathematics. The assessment of children's understanding of mathematics is examined with particular reference to recognizing misconceptions and dealing with them in a supportive way. Questioning is a powerful tool in the assessment of mathematics and the types of questions that can be helpful in generating assessment opportunities are discussed. Target-setting to inform planning leads to a discussion of planning for different age groups. The generic theme of cross-curricular planning, as mentioned in earlier chapters, is also further examined here.

It is important to ensure that all children have equal opportunities in mathematics and in Chapter 7, we explore some of the issues surrounding the accessibility of the mathematics curriculum for all children. Various groups of children who may be excluded from the curriculum will be considered. This includes children with EAL, those whose home background is culturally different from that of the classroom, those who find mathematics difficult and those who are more able than others in their classroom. We also explore practical ideas for providing suitable activities and minimizing possible barriers to learning.

The first seven chapters are largely concerned with the role of the individual class teacher or practitioner. Chapter 8, in contrast, aims to put this role more firmly within the whole school context. The role of the primary teacher or pre-school practitioner to inspire, support and challenge mathematical learning in children across the curriculum and in all areas of learning can be an intimidating one and this chapter explores how the mathematics coordinator or subject leader in the school or setting can support colleagues in this endeavour.

Mathematics as a Subject Area

INTRODUCTION

The first two chapters of this book give an overview of current research and look at how our developing knowledge about the nature of mathematics might impinge on the way that mathematics is taught within the primary school and in pre-school settings.

In this chapter we look at the way in which the understanding of mathematics as a subject has evolved over time, from a field of study which comprises sets of procedures and skills that have to be mastered and followed, to a socially situated branch of learning, much wrapped up in our day-to-day life and our society.

We will, therefore, consider:

- The nature of mathematics
- Children's mathematical understandings outside school
- How teaching and learning in school might be developed

The first section of the chapter explores some of the historical and current perceptions about the nature of mathematics, in particular noting the decline of the idea that mathematics was concerned mainly with the development of knowledge about procedures and principles and the emergence of the view that mathematics is socially situated, bound up in and inseparable from real life.

The second section examines the relationship between informal and formal mathematics, looking particularly at the mathematical understanding children might build outside school, how this might come about and the relationship between the two.

Finally we will see how current perceptions of the nature of mathematics have manifested themselves in practice and how teaching and learning in pre-school and in school might be developed in the future.

The Nature of Mathematics

In order to teach mathematics effectively we must clearly understand what the nature of mathematics is currently thought to be. Traditionally, in the first half of the twentieth century, mathematics was viewed as a set of procedures and principles that had to be taught before any potential mathematical understanding could take place. The learner then practised these mathematical principles in the form of formal mathematical exercises, usually from textbooks, until the procedures had been mastered.

 A Chance to Think

An example of mathematics for 8-year-olds
Taken from Schonell and Cracknell (1952)

Notation
You already know how to write numbers like 1, 234.
　This is read as *one thousand two hundred and thirty-four.*
　Suppose we write a number like this: 23,123.
　This is read as *twenty-three thousand one hundred and twenty-three.* You notice that the words 'twenty-three' are used twice.
　We talk about twenty-three **in the thousands** just as we talk about twenty-three **in the tens and units.**
　Now let us go another step and write 123,123.
　This reads *one hundred and twenty-three thousand one hundred and twenty-three.*
　You notice that the numbers have been repeated. In one case we call them thousands and in the other we do not.
　Our numbers are arranged IN GROUPS OF THREE:
　　Hundreds　Tens　and Units
　The first group of three are all **units** and the second group are all **thousands.**
　Now look at this:
　Here is our group of three numbers:

In the first column we put single units, just plain 'ones'.
In the second column 'T' we put 'bundles' of TEN UNITS or 'TENS'.

In the third column 'H' we put 'bundles' of ONE HUNDRED UNITS or

'HUNDREDS'.

The text continues showing three columns under the heading 'thousands' and then puts the two sets of columns side by side. This is followed by examples to complete. These comprise numbers such as *fifty-three thousand six hundred and seventy-nine* to be 'written in figures' first within the columns as described and then without columns.

Then, later, when the principles and procedures were familiar to the child, he or she was introduced to related word problems. Such problems were usually designed to practise only one type of mathematical concept at a time and any link with the student's real world was at best tenuous and at worst not even considered.

A Chance to Think

A mathematical problem (Schonell and Cracknell, 1952)

Our garden was ninety-seven yards round. The fence was made of five rows of wire. We took this away and used it to fence a field, but when we had put all the wire into one piece, it only went once round the field. How far was it round the field?

More recently this narrow view of mathematics has been superseded, not only in England but also internationally, by a more progressive view of mathematical understanding that describes mathematics as being bound up and inseparable from the experiences that we have in real life (De Lange, 1996).

England, in theory, has a long tradition of valuing applied mathematics and encouraging children to develop their mathematical problem-solving skills. The Cockcroft report in 1982, for example, described a numerate person as one who had 'an at-homeness with numbers and an ability to cope with the practical mathematical demands of everyday life' (Cockcroft, 1982, paragraph 4).

These ideals from the Cockcroft report, though, have not always been translated into classroom practice and despite the fact that the original English National Curriculum for Mathematics (1988) emphasized that open-ended and real-life problem-solving and investigations were central to mathematical learning, there has been a tendency in some English schools to teach processes first and

Planning sheet	Day One	Unit 9 *Multiplication and*
Oral and Mental		**Main Teaching**
Objectives and Vocabulary	**Teaching Activities**	**Objectives and Vocabulary**
Count on and back in steps of 2, 5 and 10.	• Count on the counting stick forwards and backwards in each of the steps 2, 5 and 10 gaining speed as you repeat the count. • Introduce 'flashing hands'. Ask the children to watch silently as 'fives' are flashed. They should count in fives in their heads and record the total on their whiteboards. • Use the grid from Resource sheet 9.1. Fold it to show different numbers of 5p coins. Ask the children to count in 5s in their heads to work out the amount shown and write it on their whiteboards. Q If you can see six 5p coins, how much money is that? How many coins are hidden? How much money is that?	Understand multiplication as repeated in addition and as an array. Read and begin to write the related vocabulary.
VOCABULARY lots of groups of		VOCABULARY multiply multiplied by lots of groups of repeated addition array rows columns
RESOURCES Counting stick Cut out grid from Resource sheet 9.1 Whiteboards		RESOURCES OHT 9.1 Whiteboards

	Year Group: *3*
	Plenary
Teaching Activities	**Teaching Activities/ Focus Questions**

Teaching Activities	Teaching Activities/ Focus Questions
• Revise multiplication as repeated addition by showing the socks illustration on OHT 9.1. **Q** How many groups of two are there? • Record this as a repeated addition sentence 2 + 2 + 2 + 2 = 8 and then as a multiplication sentence, 2 x 4 = 8, and ask the class to copy on individual whiteboards. All say together '2 multiplied by 4 equals 8'. Explain that there are 2 in each group and we multiply this by 4 to get 8. **Q** Why did we say multiplied by 4 for this picture? What if I had seven pairs of socks, what would the sentence be then? • Repeat this time showing the groups of 5p coins on OHT 9.1. Ask the children to record repeated addition sentences and multiplication sentences on their whiteboards for each group of coins. • Now show the array of 4 rows of 5 dots showing one row at a time, asking the children to count in fives. **Q** How many in each row? How many rows? • All write and read together as a repeated addition sentence; 5 + 5 + 5 + 5 = 20 and as a multiplication sentence 5 x 4 = 20. • Using the next array, demonstrate building rows of 4s. **Q** How many dots are in each row? How many rows? Record as a multiplication sentence 4 x 5 = 20. **Q** What do you notice about these two arrays/ sentences? • Rotate the arrays through 90 degrees to reinforce the 'sameness'. Point out that 4 x 5 and 5 x 4 have the same answer. **Q** What other arrays would have 20 counters in all? **Q** What arrays can you make for the number 24? • Challenge the children to work in pairs to find as many arrays with a total of 24 as they can. They should record each array and multiplication sentence in their books.	• Tell the class that you have written a multiplication sentence on a card (e.g. 4 x 6 = 24) which you are not going to show them. Say that you will draw a diagram to help them work out what it is. When they think they know, children should write the sentence on their whiteboards. Draw an array e.g. 6 rows of 4. **Q** How did you decide on your sentence? • Show your 'hidden sentence'. Explain that 6 x 4 = 24 and 4 x 6 = 24 are both right, depending whether you describe the rows or columns. • Ask the children to think of a multiplication sentence then draw the associated array on their whiteboards so that another child can guess their sentences. By the end of the lesson, children should be able to: • record mental multiplication sentences using the x and = signs; • understand multiplication as repeated addition and as describing an array. (Refer to supplement of examples, section 5, page 47.)

contextualize later (Hughes, 1986). Problem-solving and investigation have often been used as 'bolt-on' activities rather than as an integral part of everyday teaching and the child's learning. It seems that there may be a common belief in England (if we can take policy-makers' views and teachers' actions as typical) that mathematics needs to be taught in a fairly formal way separated somewhat from the real world, reliant on skills and processes rather than on realistic contexts and everyday social practices. The introduction of the English National Numeracy Strategy (DfEE, 1999), which while emphasizing much that is good, has done little to improve the situation because it has separated mathematics, at least in time, from the rest of the curriculum. It is even possible, in many classrooms, that the mathematical experiences that the children engage in have become even further narrowed because school mathematics has moved even further away from other school subjects and the children's real-life, out-of-school experiences.

Pages 8–9 show a typical unit plan taken from the English National Numeracy Strategy. It is expected that the work shown would be carried out in the autumn term of Year 3 (children aged 7–8). The plan makes no reference to the situations in which a child might use the mathematics nor attempts to suggest a context for learning. It is purely designed to teach and practise a process (ref: http://www.standards.dfes.gov.uk/ numeracy).

A more modern, enriched view suggests that, rather than treating mathematics as a discrete subject it is important to relate it to the child's everyday experiences and other areas of the taught curriculum. In order to develop a good understanding and confidence in mathematics, children need to be given the opportunity to construct mathematical meaning based on the modelling of real situations, which have a context that the children can interpret in relation to their own life experiences of mathematics. Thus mathematics not only encompasses the ability to carry out mathematical computation but is grounded in the children's need to make sense of their experiences. It is important to try to enhance children's ability to solve mathematical problems by giving them the opportunity to reason and enquire as well as to develop the ability to organize, structure and communicate their response.

Children can, for example, be encouraged to collect, record and interpret data in their own way. 'In one setting of 3- and 4-year-olds, children were responsible for collecting the choices for mid-morning staff drinks. The children took a clipboard to collect the drink choices of the staff. Then they read their information to the member of staff who made their drinks' (Worthington and Carruthers, 2003: 151).

The general belief, then, in much of Continental Europe and some of the rest of the world at least, is that mathematics (especially for the young) cannot be separated from everyday context and that it is embedded in societal values and ideals (*Te Whaarkiri*, Ministry of Education, New Zealand, 1996; Treffers and Beishuizen, 1999, and Whitburn, 1996).

In the Netherlands, for example, mathematics educators believe that their children need to be exposed to mathematical ideas that are based in real-life experiences. Teachers encourage their children to look for pattern and structure in realistic situations (Treffers and Beishuizen, 1999). They call this philosophy Dutch Realistic Mathematics and we explore this further in Chapter 2.

According to these more modern views, mathematics involves logic, investigation, questioning and the exchange of ideas. It is bound up in the notion that the understanding of abstract ideas in mathematics relies on concrete experience, reflection and experimentation. Children also need to be able to become involved in and reflect on new experiences, from many perspectives, so that they can adjust their real world continuously (De Lange, 1996) to encompass new mathematical understanding.

De Lange called this adjustment process 'conceptual mathematization'. He suggested that a cyclical schematic model for the learning process involved could be represented as:

Schematic model for the learning process

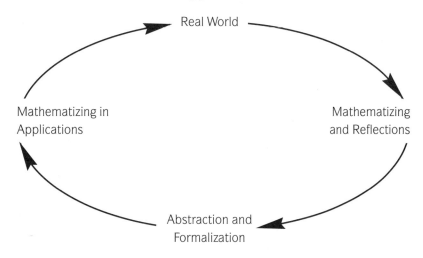

The two aspects of this model that De Lange found particularly noteworthy were:

Firstly its emphasis on concrete experience to validate and test abstract concepts. Secondly the feedback to describe a social learning and problem solving process that generates valid information to assess deviations from the desired goal. (De Lange, 1996: 57)

This view of learning attempts to draw together the informal mathematics that children engage in outside school and the formal mathematics that they will experience within school. It also endeavours to take into account the cultural significance of mathematics for the child.

Children's Outside-school Mathematical Understandings

Most of us will have noticed that even very young children have an interest in things mathematical and given the opportunity many of them will have grown familiar with the number system and developed ideas about shape, space and pattern before they even enter school and nursery. Some of this development, at least, will probably have come about within the home, for example through sharing biscuits with other members of the family or choosing how many sausages they want for tea, singing number rhymes or playing with containers in the bath. From research carried out within the home (Bottle, 2003) it seems that even very young children enjoy mathematical problem-solving and sometimes demonstrate a strong desire to understand mathematical concepts.

 A Chance to Think

Helen, aged 3, was playing with her mother with a plastic loaf of sliced bread and some plastic food .

Mum   (points to bread) That's my piece, whose is this?
         (picks up second piece of bread)
Helen   That's yours.
Mum   Oh, do I have two ham sandwiches? I will have tomato on one
         and one with lettuce.
Helen   (puts tomato on the ham and lettuce on another slice and puts
         the two together)

Mum	Oh thank you. (pretends to eat) That's lovely, that's delicious. (puts sandwich on a plate)
Helen	(puts tomato on the ham and puts on another empty slice, gives it to Mum)
Mum	Whose is this one?
Helen	Yours.
Mum	Oh, two sandwiches. (puts on another plate) Thank you.
Helen	Two and one for Helen. (makes another sandwich) Let's have butter. (pretends to spread bread, puts on lettuce and a top slice of bread, puts on a plate) Another plate.
Helen	(puts another sandwich on a plate)
Mum	Whose is that?
Helen	It's dolly's. (gets up to give to the doll)

Within this short exchange Helen demonstrated that she was able to count, share, match and sort. (Bottle, 2003)

Children do not all receive the same mathematical experiences at home, however, and even at school entry it is clear that some children understand more mathematical ideas than others. Some, for example, will know more than others about counting and simple mathematical operations such as practical addition and subtraction. It is apparent from research conducted by Aubrey (1994) that some children develop many of the skills needed to enable effective counting and some develop a deeper understanding of number in the years before school while others do not.

 ### A Chance to Think

Tim, aged 4, was making paper chains. He was competent in reciting the number sequence but had difficulty with one-to-one correspondence.

Mum	That is huge.
Tim	We can count it.
Mum	Go on then. Yours is bigger than mine.
Tim	(counts Mum's chain [not one to one]) 1,2,3,4,5,6.
Mum	Well done, yes, it is.
Tim	Mine's got (spreads out) 1,2,3,4,5,6,7,8,9,10,11,12,13,14. 14. I've got 14 [does not count accurately] That's more. (Bottle, 2003)

Although his counting skills were not always accurate he had a good understanding of what counting was for. He could count in sequence and knew that 14 was more than six.

As well as differences in the amount and type of number activity that the children have practised there also will be differences in other aspects of mathematical activity that will have been experienced at home. Shape and space are areas of mathematics, for example, that are synonymous with everyday life and activity. Everything that a child touches has shape and form and as a child moves around, he or she will be experiencing space and developing spatial awareness. Children will also be likely to come into contact with measures, mainly as comparison of length, height, volume, capacity, mass and time, and will almost certainly experience concepts such as area and speed. The opportunities for all of these mathematical experiences will vary from child to child.

 A Chance to Think

James, aged 22 months, built a bridge but his car was too tall to go through.

Mum   It won't go through it now. (picks up bridge and adds bricks to legs)

James (tries to help)

Mum   That's it, like this. (shows James how to put the bricks together and builds a taller bridge) Mum's going to make a toy bridge for your car. (puts bridge down on carpet) Ready, ready. (pushes car through the bridge)

James (picks up the bridge and removes one leg)

Mum   Mummy's poor bridge. (Bottle, 2003)

Here James was learning about shape, space and comparing measures.

While a lot of children of all ages will have a variety of experiences that are essentially mathematical at home, for many traditional outside-school mathematical activities have all but disappeared from the home agenda. With the advent of credit and debit cards, for example, carrying out transactions in shops with coins is now a novelty, and the demise of the corner shop means that experiencing activities that used to be part of everyday life now rely on the child's parent or carer making a concerted effort to seek out opportunities. Changes in lifestyle have meant that home baking has declined, giving less opportunity for children to weigh cooking ingredients, and the rise in the popularity of eating in front of the TV means that no dining table needs to be laid with plates and cutlery.

The depth of understanding that a child has about a mathematical idea and how he or she is able to use that knowledge in a variety of situations may also vary according to the social situation in which it was developed. A child who has learnt about measuring by helping his parent or carer measure and cut wood for shelves, for example, would probably have developed a better understanding of the importance of accurate measurement and correct use of measuring instruments for a variety of purposes than a child who had merely practised measuring, possibly in school, for no obvious or meaningful purpose. It may be that

the ways in which concepts are formed are of some significance. In particular, studies of the effects of Western-type schooling on cognitive development have resulted in the idea that school concepts and everyday concepts about the same conceptual field may not be the same. (Nunes, Schliemann and Carraher 1993: 49)

Learning about mathematics outside school is not just the preserve of the very young. Important research by Nunes, Schliemann and Carraher (1993), conducted on 9-year-old and 12-year-old street children in a large Brazilian city demonstrated that children involved in the 'invisible economy' selling small items on the street or market were very proficient at 'street mathematics', that is, the mathematics that they needed to carry out their small businesses.

Interviewers in the city posing as customers questioned five young street vendors. Purchases were made and discussion was carried out about cost and change. The children were later given 'school-type' problems and computation exercises involving similar arithmetic to that used in street vending. Researchers found that while the children were able to solve 98 per cent of the street mathematics they solved less than 74 per cent of the word problems and 37 per cent of the computation exercises. It was found that the children used different strategies for each situation. They used oral methods for the street mathematics, speaking as they calculated but for the 'school-type' mathematics they tried to use formal written methods. It was concluded that children develop different systems to solve street and school mathematics and that even those quite competent at culturally embedded (informal) mathematics were not always able to transfer that ability to school (formal) mathematics (Nunes *et al.*, 1993).

In this study it was found that this informal mathematics that the children engaged in out of school was not always useful to them in school. They were good at solving mathematical problems in the 'outside school' context, which they understood, but were poor at solving problems involving similar arithmetic in school. It seems that the children were unable to see the connection between the home/street and school situations and developed separate systems to solve home and school mathematics. This has important ramifications for teachers in school as it shows that children may not make connections between what are essentially the same mathematical tasks just presented in different contexts.

From this research on children's ability to connect mathematical experiences and from the research on children's home experiences described previously it seems that there are two main problems for children in pre-school or school. The first is that, although children will have some outside-school or informal mathematical understanding, the nature of this understanding will vary from child to child. The second is that there is often a gap between what they can do at home and what they are able to demonstrate in the school situation. This means that their outside-school knowledge can be underestimated or go unrecognized by their teachers (Aubrey, 1994 and 1997).

 A Chance to Think

Five-year-old Megan often chose to play in the role-play area in the classroom. She was able to lay the table, share plates, cups and cutlery between children and say how many more would be needed for everyone in the game, to have one each. This demonstrated that she was able to count, sort, match one to one, recognize pattern and do simple addition and subtraction. Her teacher was keen that she move on to simple recording but when faced with more formal activities she showed little interest in or understanding of the addition process and the use of counters or other practical apparatus did not seem to help her. Other children who appeared to have less all-round understanding had completed the first worksheets provided by the teacher with relative ease. On talking to her mother it became clear to the teacher that Megan had enjoyed role-play at home with her mother and older sibling. Her mother, because of her strong belief that school was the place for the more formal aspects of mathematics, had not introduced her to any of these. It was clear, then, that while role-play had made 'human sense' to Megan, she failed to see the point of the out-of-context activities provided by the teacher.

Transferring Mathematics from Home to School

The research by Nunes, *et al.* (1993) indicates that cultural values and practices outside school affect the mathematical development of children within school and the differences between the mathematics of home and school affect the children's ability to succeed. The problem seems to be that mathematical knowledge may 'become connected to the activities through which that knowledge is acquired' (Nunes and Bryant, 1996:104) and thus it seems that even those children quite competent at informal mathematics may be unable to transfer that ability to school if the context is unrecognized. This question of transferability between the mathematics of home and school does not, of course, occur exclusively in Brazil and it is clear in England too that there can be a considerable gap between the informal mathematics that children engage in at home and the more formal mathematics that they are expected to do in school (Aubrey, 1994). It seems that although some children may build up a high level of informal mathematical knowledge outside school, such as adding scores mentally for a card or board game, they may not be able to see the links between this and the mathematics that they encounter in school, such as being asked to add mentally six and three, which is divorced from a familiar context. This suggests that the context within which a mathematical activity or task is presented in school can have considerable impact on a child's ability to demonstrate mathematical understanding.

A Chance to Think

In a Year 1 class 5-year-old Tony had engaged in general sorting and counting activities and was just beginning to record his practical addition and subtraction tasks. This had proved to be a struggle. The use of counters did not seem to enhance his understanding of the more formal written work. Other children had completed the first worksheets in the scheme used at the school with relative ease but Tony demonstrated a lack of understanding and seemed confused about their relevance. A shop was set up in the classroom for the children to play in. It was hoped that within this experience children would become familiar with coin denomination, money use and simple addition and subtraction in a context familiar to them. The children were given real money to use, which was counted at the end of each day to make sure that it was all still in the classroom. Tony soon took charge of the money tin. He was able to distinguish between the coins, add up informally using 1-, 2- and even 5-pence pieces in the correct denomination. This seemed to go against everything that had been seen so far. Questioning Tony revealed that here was a context that made 'human sense' to him, as he was expected to do his mother's shopping at the local corner shop. The other seemingly 'more able' children in the class, though some were aware of the different denominations of the coins, were not able to add or subtract mixed coins (Bottle, 2003).

It seems, then, that because mathematics is socially constructed it would enhance children's ability to develop secure mathematical understanding if close links between in-school and out-of-school mathematics could be made. It is therefore important for teachers to know more about the mathematical practices of the home in order to appreciate how the children's mathematical understandings were acquired and developed so that they can plan for effective learning that builds on prior knowledge.

There is also some evidence that children's development of mathematical competence within school may be associated with the expectations and attitudes of their parents. Parental attitude may affect the children's enthusiasm for mathematical activity and the effort that they put into achieving understanding (Kwok and Lytton, 1996; Stevenson *et al.*, 1990; Uttal, Lummis and Stevenson, 1988). It is thought that high expectations and encouragement by parents may lead to higher achievement of the child, while low expectations and lack of encouragement may lead to complacency, which can reduce the child's motivation.

Stevenson *et al.* (1990) tested the children in two classes in each of 20 Chicago schools and two classes in each of 11 Beijing schools for mathematical competence. They also interviewed the children's parents and found that many parents of the North American children tended to regard low attainment as lack of aptitude for mathematics. The East Asian parents, on the other hand, had high expectations of their children's attainment in mathematics. American parents were apparently easily satisfied with their children's progress and had 'excessively positive attitudes' (Stevenson *et al.*, 1990) towards their achievements.

In some countries, including England, there seems to be a lack of emphasis and even interest, outside school, in the importance of children's mathematical development. One of the reasons for this may be that it is not widely accepted that mathematical experiences are just as important as literacy experiences (Munn and Schaffer, 1993) and numerous teachers in England are able to cite anecdotal evidence from discussion with parents and carers suggesting that many parents are more worried about the development of reading and writing than the growth of mathematical understanding. Another reason for lack of emphasis may be that while adults use number skills effectively in the course of everyday activities, they tend not to regard such number activities as mathematics.

A Chance to Think

Charles's mother was a cook in an old people's home but she did not recognize that there was any mathematics in her job, even though she was expected to adapt recipes for the number of residents and to keep account of her spending. She described this work as 'financial' (Bottle, 2003).

Furthermore, it may be that literacy activities are associated with leisure by the vast majority of adults and they are often prepared to engage even very small children in their own literacy activities. Very few adults, on the other hand, see numbers as 'objects of play' (Paulos, 1991: 3). Children are often encouraged, at home, to play with words such as rhyming nonsense words and are allowed to use their own interpretations of language construction, for example the child may verbalize the past tense of the verb 'thought' as 'thinked'. This type of 'mistake' is often interpreted as developmental and therefore goes uncorrected. 'Mistakes' in counting, however, are rarely allowed to go uncorrected even when the child has invented his or her own version of a sequential pattern such as 'twenty-ten' for 'thirty'.

 A Chance to Think

Sally, aged 3 called her elbow 'armbell' and for a long time her parents were quite happy for her to continue to use her own interpretation as a representation of this part of her body and considered it 'cute'. When she used 'ten-teen' to represent twenty, however, she was immediately corrected.

The beliefs and attitudes of parents and carers, then, can have considerable effect on the children's development throughout school; if we add to this differing beliefs about the place of mathematics in life in general and at home in particular this can generate considerable variation in children's experiences and therefore understanding.

How Teaching and Learning in School Might Be Developed

It is widely accepted that learning mathematics is important if children are to understand fully the world in which they live. In order to be numerate children need to develop logic such as understanding in counting, not only the ordinal nature of counting but also the relationship between numbers. They also need to learn about conventional systems such as the number system, which allows for mathematical communication, and to use their mathematical thinking meaningfully and appropriately and know which mathematical technique to use in a new situation (Nunes and Bryant, 1996: 4–17).

Elements of the Nunes and Bryant's criteria for being numerate can be seen, for example, in the responses of very young children.

 A Chance to Think

Tim, aged 28 months, could use his mathematical thinking meaningfully and appropriately.

Tim	Mum, you have one. (biscuit)
Mum	One more.
Tim	One more. (throws)
Mum	Oh, thank you.
Tim	And one for Tim.
Mum	One for Tim.

Dan, aged 3, knew the mathematical techniques that he could use in a new situation:

Dan   (watches marbles in marble run) If you put two down it goes down (lets two go) and if you put two more down it makes four and stops there. (lets two more go) (Bottle, 2003)

It is important that teachers and practitioners give children many opportunities to apply mathematical concepts in and to a variety of contexts because it is this that gives the children the chance to develop an understanding of the structure of mathematical knowledge. This is essential, as, according to Nunes and Bryant (1996: 234)

Mathematics is generative. Children do not have to learn every bit of mathematics that they have to know. If they understand how mathematical knowledge is structured, they can generate knowledge they have not learned.

Lack of opportunity to use mathematical thinking in a wide variety of contexts may affect children's ability to apply mathematics in novel contexts that they will meet later in their school career and in their everyday life.

Giving children a wide range of experiences in a variety of contexts is likely to develop their secure understanding of the relationships between mathematical ideas, the significance of what they are doing and the associations between mathematics and other areas of learning. Those children who are restricted to one mode of learning, such as playing formal mathematical games or completing endless mathematical worksheets, will have such opportunities severely limited.

We now go on to explore how we might relate school mathematics work to children's out-of-school understanding. Linking home and school mathematics is an important start to developing children's formal logical thinking, which, many believe, facilitates true mathematical understanding.

Children as they mature need to be able to move from contextual, metaphoric understanding to abstract mathematical thinking. To do so they need to be able to construct reasoned argument about mathematical principles. This in turn requires the support of a more experienced other who can engage with the learner in challenging discussions about mathematical ideas.

Children develop their understanding of mathematics not only through interaction with materials but also through socially mediated practices in contexts that make sense to them. Children need the opportunity to work through problems in order to develop an abstract conceptualization of the mathematics involved. The weight of current research suggests that the experienced other is likely to help the child in developing mathematical understanding as long as their interaction is appropriate and challenging.

Bruner (1986) believed that appropriate instruction is required to transform a child's spontaneous activity into symbolic, rational thinking and develop his or her understanding of mathematical concepts and relationships. Similarly Rogoff (1990: 39) said:

novices actively attempt to make sense of new situations and may even be primarily responsible for putting themselves in the position to learn. At the same time, their partners who have relatively greater skill and understanding can often more easily find effective ways to achieve shared thinking that stretch the less skilled partner's understanding.

Schaffer and Liddell (1984) observed 16 nursery nurses working with both individual and groups of children on a simple construction task. It was found that one-to-one interaction between adult and child was more effective than interaction between one adult and a number of children simultaneously. It was concluded that this was because one-to-one contact allowed for sustained interaction between adult and child whereas polyadic contact led to fragmented interaction. The quality of interaction and therefore thinking, then, can be enhanced if children are given opportunities at times to work one to one with an adult.

If in addition an adult working with a child can identify the elements of a task that a child can accomplish alone and at the same time recognize the elements of the task that he or she could achieve with some assistance, then that adult will be able to support the child effectively in his or her learning (Wood and Middleton, 1975). Response is also better when an adult guides a child through a task rather than doing it for him or her, drawing connections between what the child already knows and new learning and understanding, gradually 'shifting the responsibility' (Radziszewska and Rogoff, 1988: 846) on to the child as he or she became more competent.

The effective teacher will therefore be able to recognize which aspect of a task the child needs help with at the moment. This could be help to begin a task, support for the child as the task is executed or helping the child to verbalize what he or she has achieved at the end. In this way the adult supports the child's emerging skills while they are practised, scaffolding only to the extent that it is deemed necessary and helpful to move the child's understanding forward. It is not always easy in the classroom to arrange this kind of one-to-one support because of the obvious demands on the teacher, and in a busy classroom children who are considered to be competent at mathematics are sometimes left to get on by themselves. This will not, however, in the long run help them to develop the abstract conceptualization of the mathematics that is so important for later progress.

 A Chance to Think

Some research conducted by Rogoff demonstrated that when working with toddlers on puzzles 'mothers often began by ensuring that their children perceived the puzzle in the same way they did (as a truck), by asking the children to identify the overall array and its pieces'. This establishment of shared understanding enabled the mothers to refer to the pieces with the terms such as wheels and headlights that both partners recognized and that related the pieces to the whole. Children will 'stretch to understand the interpretation available in interaction with their caregivers and companions'. (Rogoff, 1990: 74)

Effective teaching requires that children are actively engaged in participating in shared experiences with more experienced others. Some researchers describe this mediated and active role of the learner in culturally organized mathematical activity as that of apprenticeship (Anderson, 1991 and 1993; Bruner, 1983; Rogoff, 1990; Wells, 1979; and Young, 1996). This approach to learning gives children opportunities to think things through and to communicate with themselves on a thinking level, as well as being given the chance to discuss their thinking with others.

Primary school classrooms and pre-school settings can vary in the quality and quantity of mathematical activity in which their children have the opportunity to engage but it is clear that where the children have the opportunity to engage in mathematical activity in contextually relevant situations with the support of a more experienced adult or even child, their interest is maintained for longer and therefore their learning is likely to be enhanced. Munn and Schaffer (1993: 71) concluded, from their research involving ten Scottish nurseries, that 'when children received adult support the children's interest in numeracy artefacts was extended and they were likely to continue what they were doing for a longer period of time'.

It should be remembered, however, that any adult and child exchanges may vary in quality. This is because the quality of interaction largely depends on the mathematical understanding, intentions and cultural setting of the adult (Wertsch, 1994), whether that adult is the child's parent or his or her teacher.

This idea of mathematical understanding developing through activity that is embedded in everyday contexts is not a new one. Donaldson, for example, argued as long ago as 1978 that young children learn best in contextualized situations.

There has recently been a shift away from formalized and abstract mathematical activity for our youngest pupils in England, as the new Foundation Stage Curriculum for children aged 3 to 5 emphasizes the importance of play. This is significant in terms of the children's mathematical development as through play children can create contexts for learning mathematics that are both relevant and interesting to them and rich in opportunity for mathematical concepts and relationships to be explored. Foundation stage practitioners need, however, to think carefully about what opportunities for play are created for the children, how these are organized and the adult role. Any adult contribution and intervention related to children's play must be sensitively constructed to maximize the children's participation and mathematical learning while avoiding moving the emphasis away from the child's interest.

Using mathematics in practical, contextualized situations often allows the child to make links between mathematical areas. Here is an example.

A Chance to Think

Anna, aged 4, was playing with some soft toys and a washing basket with a variety of toys in it.

Anna   (to her mother) Yes, Cotton Tail (toy rabbit), let's see, he doesn't have any arm bands does he? Ahaa, here's two things that can be another rabbit's arm bands, can't they? Ahaa, take this one off, see, and put the other one on. Now he has two hearts.

Mum   A pair of hearts.

Anna   Yes, but Cotton Tail's out at the moment.

Mum   He's gone for a swim, has he?

Anna   No, not at the moment, no, he's not at sea at the moment, he won't get wet (looks through a box of toys). I just have to look through and take the things I need, yes, mats, and I need some money, put the money there (puts on the arm of a chair).

Mum   How much money have you got?

Anna   1, 2, 3, 4 yes, 1, 2, 3 and 4 (holds up coins). I've got one of this sort and two of these and one of these.

Mum   Are there any the same?

Anna   Yes, these two are the same.

Mum   And what number have they got on there? (points to coin)

Anna   Both two and that one's got one and that's a zero (picks up rabbit), but Cotton Tail can't go for a swim cause he hasn't got any armbands, but he (points to another toy, sorts through toys) can cause he has. Aha, here's some more money, I got some more money (puts with the rest).

This sequence demonstrates the child's experience of cardinal number, using the counting sequence, one-to-one correspondence, recognition of numerals, shape, matching and coin recognition, all within one activity (Bottle, 2003).

In England the formalization of the mathematics curriculum for the 3- to 5-year-olds has been relaxed but giving children contextually rich mathematical opportunity should not be confined to our youngest children. It is just as important that children of all ages are given the opportunities to both develop mathematical understanding through their own chosen context and through relevant and interesting contexts chosen by the teacher.

A Chance to Think

A class of 7-year-olds at a local primary school, for example, were preparing for Christmas. They had decided that they would like to make small Christmas puddings, one for each of them. They decided that they could cook each of them in a mug that they could bring from home. The teacher had a recipe for a pudding that would fit into a 1-litre pudding basin. Some of the children worked out, by measuring, how many mugs were equivalent to a 1-litre basin. They found that five small puddings could be made from the recipe for the 1-litre basin. There were 30 children in the class, so some of the children worked out how much of each given ingredient would be needed in order to make enough mixture to fill all of the mugs. Children also had to cut lining paper and work out cooking times. The task was carried out successfully and all children had a small pudding to take home for Christmas.

It is important that teachers and other practitioners recognize and incorporate the principles evident in the children's natural learning experiences, such as day-to-day classroom routines and activity, not only during the pre-school years but also beyond. These mathematical experiences could include the encouragement of play based mathematical activity, building on mathematics in a context that the child has chosen and that is relevant to that child and the exploration of mathematical pattern and structures through investigations and problem solving. Enhanced understanding of the mathematics that children are likely to engage in outside school might help develop practitioners' ability to link mathematical work to children's everyday life because the 'more informed our vision of mathematical literacy is the more effective is its actualisation in classroom praxis' (Anderson, 1997: 57).

If play and other socially constructed activities, such as class routines, are to be used as a basis for mathematical learning then it is important that practitioners are able to recognize a mathematical idea within a child's existing activities and use them as a basis for exploration (Anning and

Edwards, 1999; Young-Loveridge, 1987). Anning and Edwards, from their study in the UK, which involved 20 practitioners undertaking small case studies in a variety of pre-school settings, suggested that 'knowing the mathematics available in an experience is a crucial factor in the guidance that an adult can give' (p. 131) and 'the learning outcomes for children that emerge from mathematical experiences will depend, in part at least, on how adults manage the support they provide so that a child can participate mathematically in an experience that has mathematical potential' (p. 126).

It is clear, then, that teachers and practitioners need to have mathematics on their minds the whole time, just as they do language at present. They need to look for and use every opportunity for mathematical development and utilize naturally occurring mathematical play, activity and talk to link mathematics to real life. The relationships between different areas of learning, both in school and out, should be explored, not just within mathematics but between subjects so that the relevance of mathematics is made more obvious and so that children are able to understand the contexts in which the mathematics that they learn can be used.

Summary

In this chapter we have looked at how views of mathematics have changed over time: once viewed as a set of principles, mathematics is now seen as part of everyday life, wrapped up in culture and social practices.

We have also recognized that children come to school with different levels of understanding and varying attitudes that need to be taken into account when assessing their understanding and in planning a suitable curriculum for each class. The mathematics of everyday life is not always seen to be linked to the practices in school and this creates a gap. Understanding better the mathematical practices that children are engaged in outside school may help us to bridge that gap.

The part that adults or more experienced others play in providing opportunities for mathematical development seems to be important and children benefit from being taught in a supportive atmosphere with more knowledgeable others who can scaffold their learning, through mediation and discussion, at an appropriate level within contextual and interest-related tasks.

Reflective Questions

- What do you believe to be the nature of mathematics?
- Do you engage in mathematics in your day-to-day life? Try to think of five mathematical experiences that you have had today.
- What are your attitudes towards mathematics?
- How can you develop your mathematics teaching to minimize the home–school gap?

REFERENCES AND FURTHER READING

Anderson, A. (1991) 'Learning mathematics at home: a case study', *Canadian Children*, 16 (2) 47–58.

Anderson, A. (1993) 'Wondering: one child's questions and mathematics learning', *Canadian Children*, 18 (2) 26–30.

Anderson, A. (1997) 'Families and mathematics: a study of parent–child interactions', *Journal for Research in Mathematics Education*, 28 (4) 484–511.

Anning, A. and Edwards, A. (1999) *Promoting Children's Learning from Birth to Five: Developing the New Early Years Professional.* Buckingham: Open University Press.

Aubrey, C. (1994) 'An investigation of children's knowledge of mathematics at school entry and the knowledge their teachers hold about teaching and learning mathematics: about young learners and mathematical subject knowledge', *British Educational Research Journal*, 20 (1) 105–21.

Aubrey, C. (1997) 'Children's early learning of number in school and out', in Thompson, I. (ed.) *Teaching and Learning Early Number*, Buckingham: Open University Press.

Bottle, G. (2003) 'Young children's mathematical experiences within the home', unpublished PhD thesis, University of Kent, Canterbury Christ Church University College.

Bruner, J. (1983) *Child's Talk: Learning to Use Language*, Oxford: Oxford University Press.

Bruner, J. (1986) *Actual Minds Possible Worlds*, London: Harvard University Press.

Cockcroft, W. (1982) *Mathematics Counts: Report of the Commission of Enquiry into the Teaching of Mathematics in Schools*, London: HMSO.

De Lange, J. (1996) 'Using and applying mathematics in education', in Bishop, A. (ed.) *International Handbook of Mathematics Education*, Netherlands: Kluwer Academic Publishers.

DfEE (1999) *The National Curriculum.*

DFEE (1999) *The National Numeracy Strategy.*

Donaldson, M. (1978) *Children's Minds*, London: Fontana.

Hughes, M. (1986) *Children and Number*, Oxford: Blackwell Publishers.

Kwok, D. and Lytton H. (1996) 'Perceptions of mathematics, ability versus actual mathematics performance: Canadian and Hong Kong Chinese children', *British Journal of Educational Psychology*, 66, 209–22.

Ministry of Education (1996) *Te Whaakiri: early childhood curriculum*, Wellington: New Zealand: Learning Media.

Munn, P. and Schaffer, H. (1993) 'Literacy and numeracy events in social interactive contexts', *International Journal of Early Years Education*, 1 (3), 61–80.

Nunes, T. and Bryant, P. (1996) *Children Doing Mathematics*, London: Blackwell.

Nunes, T., Schliemann, A. and Carraher, D. (1993) *Street Mathematics and School Mathematics* New York: Cambridge University Press.

Paulos, J. (1991) *Beyond Numeracy*, London: Viking.

Radziszewska, B. and Rogoff, B. (1988) 'Influence of adult and peer collaborators on children's planning skills', *Developmental Psychology*, 24, 840–8.

Rogoff, B. (1990) *Apprenticeship in Thinking: Cognitive Development in Social Context*, New York: Oxford University Press.

Schaffer, H. and Liddell, C. (1984) 'Adult–child interaction under dyadic and polyadic conditions', *British Journal of Developmental Psychology*, 2, 33–42.

Schonell F.J. and Cracknell, S.H. (1952) *Arithmetic Book 4*, London, Oliver and Boyd.

Stevenson, H., Lee, S., Chen, C., Stigler, J., Hsu, C. and Kitamura, S. (1990) 'Mathematics achievement of children in China and the United States', *Child Development*, 61, 1053–66.

Treffers, A. and Beishuizen, J.J. (1999) 'Realistic mathematics education in the Netherlands', in Thompson, I. (ed.) *Issues in Teaching Numeracy in Primary Schools*, Buckingham: Open University Press.

Uttal, D., Lummis, M. and Stevenson, H. (1988) 'Low and high mathematics achievement in Japanese, Chinese and American elementary-school children', *Developmental Psychology*, 24, 335–42.

Wells, G. (1979) *The Meaning Makers: Children Learning Language and Using Language to Learn,* London: Hodder and Stoughton.

Wertsch, J. (1994) 'The zone of proximal development: some conceptual issues', in Rogoff, B. and Wertsch, J. (eds) *Children's Learning in the Zone of Proximal Development: New Directions for Child Development*, San Francisco: Jossey-Bass.

Whitburn, J. (1996) 'Contrasting approaches to the acquisition of mathematical skills: Japan and England', *Oxford Review of Education*, 22 (4), 415–34.

Wood, D. and Middleton, D. (1975) 'A study of assisted problem solving', *British Journal of Psychology*, 66, 181–91.

Worthington, M. and Carruthers, E. (2003) *Children's Mathematics: Making Marks, Making Meaning*, London: Paul Chapman Publishing.

Young, J. (1996) 'Young children's apprenticeship in number', unpublished PhD thesis, University of North London.

Young-Loveridge, J. (1987) 'Learning mathematics', *British Journal of Developmental Psychology*, 5 (2), 155–67.

Enhancing Children's Understanding of Mathematics

INTRODUCTION

As the previous chapter has shown us, children's mathematical learning is inseparable from real life. In this chapter we will look at the links between the theory and practical mathematics in the classroom and discuss the importance of contextualizing mathematics and of providing the most successful mathematical learning environments. We will draw on research and practical experience from a variety of different countries.

We will look in detail at:

- Making mathematics meaningful
- Realistic Mathematics Education (RME) in the Netherlands
- Using the environment
- Cross-curricular mathematics
- ICT and mathematics
- Specific activities that can be designed to link mathematics to the real world
- Imagery
- Mathematics and problem solving – the Japanese example

This chapter will also focus on children using and applying their mathematical knowledge, including the development of their mathematical thinking and cover the benefits of using a variety of different settings to stimulate mathematical understanding. These will include investigations, games, problem-solving, stories and the environment. The importance of building up mental images to help children in their mathematical work will also become clear.

Making Mathematics Meaningful

Mathematical learning can be said to have taken place when children find that the mathematics they do has meaning. They may not always recognize this themselves and indeed even adults do not always recognize their own mathematical understanding. Adults who might otherwise describe themselves as poor at mathematics find no problem in applying mathematical skills that are used for a purpose in everyday life.

 A Chance to Think

Jack and Sam, for example, were very good at adding and subtracting mentally. They demonstrated their abilities when at the local pub with a group of friends practising for a forthcoming match. Jack and Sam stepped forward for their game. They each started with a score of 501 and needed to reach zero. Jack threw three darts. He landed a treble 16, a double 8 and a 17 and quickly worked out that he was now on 420. As the game closed out Sam needed 61 to win. He threw a double 20, a 7 and then knew he needed a double 7 to win the match. Unfortunately he got only a 4 but this did not worry him, as he knew that all he needed to throw next turn was a double 5. These players showed that they were mentally able to double and treble all numbers from 1 to 20, work out quick subtraction from 501 using numbers up to 180, work out the combinations needed to end on zero from any number < 161, using three darts and ending on a double.

Jane and Mike used the different context of a card game for demonstrating their mathematical ability. Jane, who was in her 70s was playing cribbage with her husband, Mike. They took turns to play their cards, always looking to find a card to make a total up to 31. Mike put down a card to make a pair. When they added up their scores they looked for sequences, doubles and combinations of cards that made 15. They demonstrated that they knew their number bonds to 31 and were able to work out combinations of two or more cards to total 15.

Mathematical skills are useful to everyone, not only for leisure pursuits but also for day-to-day living and for organizing daily, weekly and yearly finances or in estimating measures. It is surprising just how much mathematics we do without realizing it. Mundane everyday tasks from making tea to catching the correct bus for work in the morning require the ability to engage in mathematical thinking.

Sometimes quite complex tasks are carried out by people who would probably not describe themselves as mathematicians. Ranjit, for example, wanted to make some new curtains for her living room. She read in a book that she needed two and a half times the window width in order to make her curtains full enough. The actual width of the window was 120 cm and the length was 150 cm. By taking half the width of the window and multiplying it by two and a half she worked out that each curtain would need to be 150 cm in width (luckily this was the width of the fabric that she had chosen). She knew that she needed two curtains and she realized that she would need to add 20 cm to the length of each curtain to allow for the heading and a hem. Thus she worked out that she would need 340 cm of material. The material that she chose was plain; had it been patterned she would also have had to work out the extra fabric needed for a pattern match.

Similarly children also can use mathematics in everyday life. Working out the school timetable, tidying their bedroom, even getting dressed in the morning require mathematical skills such as sorting, matching, problem-solving, being able to tell the time and sequencing.

 A Chance to Think

Avais was particularly lucky as his parents thought that it was important for him to have a space in the garden of his own to take care of, so that he could engage in some problem-solving in a non-threatening environment and develop some independence. They may or may not have been aware of the mathematical possibilities that this allowed Avais to explore. His parents decided to give Avais his own small flowerbed in their garden. He dug it over and then had to decide which plants to buy and how to arrange them. He looked carefully at the plot so that he could decide how many he needed of each of his chosen flowers. He then went to the garden centre to buy the plants out of an allowance that his parents had given him. In this activity he demonstrated that he was able to estimate the area of the plot, accurately estimate how many plants he needed to fill the plot, read the prices of the packets of seeds and on the plants and work out if he had enough money to buy what he wanted, by adding their totals and subtracting this from the amount of money he had.

Problem-solving is perhaps at the heart of mathematics and it is the principal reason for its use in real life. Giving children a real context for their problem-solving gives them the best opportunity to become fluent in using mathematical skills and procedures. If we also make mathematics meaningful for children by relating it to their interests, then they will be more likely to see its relevance and use. Interestingly, in England there are moves to focus the statutory tests given to children at 11 and 7 years more closely on problem-solving skills. Perhaps this indicates that policy-makers are beginning to realize the need for mathematics to be linked to real life and make 'human sense' (Atkinson, 1995).

Realistic Mathematics Education (RME)

As we have seen, for young children especially, mathematics should not be separated from the everyday context. One country that has taken this idea on board is the Netherlands and their success in recent international comparisons has demonstrated the usefulness of their approach.

In the Netherlands young children have performed well in recent international mathematics tests. In 1995, 26 countries took part in the Third International Mathematics and Science Survey (TIMSS). Nine-year-old children in the Netherlands topped the scores from all the other European countries participating. For example Scotland came 16th and England 17th. It is interesting that in the Netherlands many children learn much of their mathematics through real-life problem-solving. The name given to this style of mathematical education is Realistic Mathematics.

As Treffers and Beishuizen (1999) point out there are two types of learning embodied by RME, named respectively 'horizontal' and 'vertical' mathematization. The former denotes the mathematics learning that evolves from engaging with real-life problems. The latter refers to the development of particular mathematical skills within the context of a realistic problem. Children develop their skills, moving from lower-level strategies to higher-level strategies, while engaging with a problem. The teacher focuses particularly on this upward development. An example of this upward development might be a child learning to count using a 'count on' strategy instead of a 'count all' strategy while counting groups of animals in a play farm. A further example could be a child learning to chunk in groups of ten rather than groups of two when using simple multiplication to work out how many coloured pencils will be needed for a group of children in the class. This two-pronged approach is very different from the mathematics teaching in many other countries where children are taught specific skills and then afterwards are encouraged to develop and use them within problem-solving contexts. This has been the practice, for example, in the United Kingdom.

Realistic Mathematics Education is underpinned by the view of Hans Freudenthal that mathematics is a human activity (Lange, 2003). However 'realistic' does not just mean real-life situations. The name is taken from the Dutch word 'zich REALISEren' which can mean 'to realise' or 'to imagine' (Heuvel-Panhuizen, 2001). Therefore contexts that are realistic to children (although imaginary) are included. This means, for example, that using stories can be useful in relating mathematical ideas to young children. Similarly games, television, videos and films can be considered as meaningful environments within which to develop mathematical learning, as can sporting events such as football matches or the Olympic Games. All of these environments become real in a child's imagination as they act them out.

 A Chance to Think

Children respond well to contexts that are meaningful to them.
The first example is of young children learning to count.

Anna and Peter were engaged in mathematical play in a corner of the classroom. They were walking model people and animals up and down a small block of wooden steps. As they did this they were counting forwards and backwards. Each count was related to either a step up or a step down. This prepared them for a later introduction to a number line.

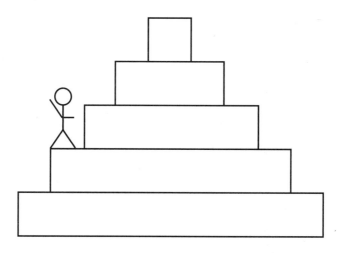

The second example demonstrates how young children can engage in tasks that include simple addition and subtraction.

A group of young children were pushing a toy bus along a track. The track was drawn out on a large map of a small town, laid out on the classroom floor. At the first bus stop the children put some play people on their bus. They continued their game with people getting on or getting off at each bus stop. The teacher joined with the children and related the play to simple addition and subtraction, the children counting the numbers on the bus after each change. Later this experience was linked to recorded work, where the children recorded these simple sums using pictures of buses and bus stops. Simple addition and subtraction had been made meaningful through concrete experience.

This example shows how older children can still be working in a realistic context even with more complicated mathematical ideas. These children were trying to get to grips with repeated addition leading to multiplication.

All the children in a class were given large sheets of paper and sticky shapes. The teacher encouraged them to design flower gardens by arranging the flowers in groups of specific numbers of their own choice, such as four or six. The children counted the flowers in their gardens using repeated addition, which was then linked to multiplication. The teacher used the different gardens created by the children as her teaching aids.

In our final example children are working on a combination of mathematical operations.

A class of 10-year-olds was engaged in planning a journey to neighbouring towns. They used local rail and bus timetables, which were spread out on their desks. The children worked out the different lengths of the journeys when taken at different times of the day or on the different types of transport. They also costed their journeys and contrasted off peak and full charge costs. The following week the children used holiday brochures to plan their dream holiday. Their desks were covered with brochures and, working in small groups, they chose and compared three different holidays of their own choice. They looked at cost, contrasting holidays that were all-inclusive and those that were not. They also looked at travel times and convenience. The teacher used the materials and learning environments to teach groups of children or the whole class effective ways of carrying out the calculations. She also used whole-class discussion to work on estimation skills.

Using the Environment

Another way to make mathematics meaningful to children is to use the indoor and outdoor environment. This can help children to relate the things around them and their everyday experiences to the mathematics that they are asked to do in school. It is an exciting and stimulating way for the children to learn and caters to the different learning styles that they may favour. Linking mathematics to the environment particularly helps children who learn best through visual stimuli. They are able, for example, to link the words 'horizontal' and 'vertical' to horizontal and vertical lines that they see around them, such as windows, beams or the side of a whiteboard in the classroom, the shelf for holding books in the school library, the guttering, down pipes and roofs of the school building or the edge of the pavement outside the school grounds.

With some pre-planning and thought, lessons outside the classroom can provide a wealth of mathematical material.

Jon and Jas went on a walk to explore the local neighbourhood with their class. Their teacher wanted to link this walk to the topic of tessellation, which she was going to cover with her class the next day. The children were asked to identify the shapes that they could see around them. Jon and Jas found circles in car wheels and plant pots, squares in windows and on notice boards, rectangles in doors and fences and parallelograms on the roof tiling. There were triangles on gable ends and semicircles at the tops of some of the doors. After some time the teacher grouped the children together to look closely at a brick wall. The children noticed that it was made up of many rectangles fitted closely together with no gaps. She then encouraged them to look for other similar patterns and they identified wooden fences, roof tiling and the pavement. They noticed that there were no repeating patterns that included circles or semicircles. The teacher encouraged the children to follow up their investigations for homework and they found tiling in their bathrooms and kitchens. Next day in class their teacher drew on their experiences to explore tessellation and tiling.

Work that utilizes the local environment, both inside and outside, can also help pupils who are predominantly kinaesthetic learners, since the children can touch, feel and actively explore the environment. For example, they can walk down a stairway and count the steps, use gardening to learn about volume, capacity and area or collect door numbers to look at sequencing and odd and even.

Chloe's teacher, for example, took her class on a visit to their local parish church. The children had visited the church each year that they had been at the school. On previous occasions Chloe had explored the church for the different shapes that could be found there and had developed her counting skills by tallying the different features such as windows, graves and pews. On this visit the children took measuring tools, such as 10 cm and metre rules, long measuring tapes and trundle wheels, and used them to take accurate measurements of the church building and also of the different features inside such as the font and the altar table. The children recorded all their results either on paper or by speaking into tape recorders. Back in school the teacher helped them to use this information to construct accurate scale drawings and subsequently models both of the church and its contents. One group of children made a large 3D model of the church and other children made accurate models of the different features that could be found inside. The children's model was admired by parents and governors at the next open afternoon.

Often when we use the environment, any mathematical work we do naturally becomes cross-curricular but it is also possible to plan deliberately to include mathematics in the whole curriculum.

Cross-curricular Mathematics

It is important for children to have experiences of using mathematics within other areas of learning because:

... It is through using mathematics in the context of other subjects that pupils develop their ability to apply mathematics. (Coles and Copeland, 2002: 7)

If mathematics can be linked to other areas of the curriculum or of learning, either at school or pre-school, then children may find it will become more meaningful to them. If they realize, for example, that they are using calculation skills when they work out how many spoons they need for their group of friends, how long a king reigned, the amount of rainfall in a season or the real distance from one town to another as represented on a map, then their interest in acquiring such calculation skills may increase.

During a designated mathematics lesson Mark was teaching his class about symmetry. He decided that while the children in his class were getting to grips with the idea of symmetry, they did not really understand its place in the real world. He decided, therefore, to take them on a walk around the school and playground area to look for symmetrical patterns. The children each carried paper and pencils so that they could sketch any patterns that they found. They looked at walls and roofs, at panes of glass in the windows, the patterns on flower heads and many more. By the end of the session each child had a collection of his or her own drawings that showed symmetrical patterns. Mark and the children then returned to the classroom and the children continued to work on symmetry with a surer understanding of its place in the real world.

There are two different approaches that can be taken to cross-curricular mathematics. First, where mathematics is taught as a discrete subject, teachers can try to find links with other topics and cultural knowledge, links that can be neglected in some learning environments. In some classrooms and pre-school settings the daily mathematics lesson is treated as stand-alone and can seem to be divorced from other subjects rather than being integrated into the rest of the curriculum or within play situations. However, the most effective teachers can and do make cross-curricular links to other areas of learning and other subjects, taking the opportunity within any mathematics lesson or activity to convey them to the children. Too often, unfortunately, in school and in pre-school settings, mathematics is seen as a distinct subject unrelated to the outside world and other interests.

 A Chance to Think

The teacher in Red Class was aware that the children needed to understand how mathematics related to the real world. In a mathematics lesson, therefore she encouraged Louise, Katy and Sam to analyse some simple data they had collected in a science lesson about themselves and the rest of their class. They made a tally chart of the different hair colours of all their classmates. They also tallied the different eye colours. They then recorded the data in two bar charts, compared the two charts and wrote down their findings. Their teacher discussed their findings with them and pointed out how they had used their numeracy skills to help them with their problem-solving in science.

A second approach is to find the mathematics in the other subjects that are taught or in other areas of learning. When planning themes or topics for their classes, teachers or practitioners can make a mind map of all the mathematics that they think can be incorporated into the children's work. The mathematics then becomes part of a holistic programme of work. If links are to be made in this way, however, then more responsibility lies with the teachers to ensure that many areas of the mathematics curriculum are covered. It may be necessary to think more creatively to ensure this is the case. Teachers will also need to point out to the children where mathematics is being used so that the children will actually identify it. Otherwise they may not make the links with meaningful situations themselves.

 A Chance to Think

Donald wanted the 8-year-olds he teaches to develop an understanding of the place of mathematics in the real world. He was planning to work with them this term on the topic of the ancient Egyptians. When planning the work he identified as much mathematics as he could within the subject area. He identified:

- A time line from that period of history through to the modern day
- 3D shapes, in particular pyramids
- Egyptian multiplication, using doubling
- The cubit

He mapped this against the class long-term plan so as to identify any gaps in mathematical knowledge that he would need to plug in some other way to ensure that the children attained the expected breadth of mathematical experience.

ICT and Mathematics

There is no doubt that children's interest in and familiarity with ICT can be used as a motivating force in learning. In their report for the DfE, Passey, Rogers, Machell and McHugh (2004) wrote that 'the motivational profiles obtained from the quantitative survey demonstrated the existence of a highly positive set of motivational characteristics in the schools in this study.' ICT is now an integral part of most children's worlds, so using it to access mathematics will make further links between this subject, other areas of learning and the real world.

 *A Chance to Think*

Mathematical work in other subjects helps children to see the usefulness of mathematics in real life. Mike and Finlay were investigating the temperature of different environments in their science work. They used a data-logging program to see the rise and fall in temperature over a period of time. They then interpreted the data by looking at the different graphs produced by the software.

The range of ICT available to teachers will vary from school to school and even from classroom to classroom, but most children will have the opportunity to work with tape recorders, computers, calculators and modelling aids such as the robotic turtle (for a more comprehensive list see the section on managing ICT in Chapter 5). ICT can be used to enhance children's mathematical learning, particularly when the tasks are thoughtfully planned to relate to real-world problems or to children's particular interests. Children often find using ICT motivating and exciting.

Using mathematical ideas gathered from outside, children may come up with ways of modelling real situations in a computer-based environment.

Jo, Stacy and Mark, for example, had been studying castles in their topic work. As part of this study they went to visit a local castle with a maze. They had great pleasure in exploring this maze and were eager to make one as part of their project. Their teacher had encouraged them in this and they had made a small maze that they wanted their classmates to explore. However, since the maze itself was only small, each child explored it by instructing a turtle towards the middle. This involved them in estimation, programming and using turns of 90 degrees. The mathematics was integral to the activity and was complementary to solving the task.

The use of ICT in a real situation can be particularly helpful.

 A Chance to Think

Indura and Aisha, both aged 7, were asked by their teacher to get a message to the school secretary using the floor turtle. The children typed and printed the note from the computer. They attached the note to the floor turtle and programmed it to reach the school office. They also programmed in a signal to alert the secretary to the turtle's arrival. The secretary was surprised to receive a message in this way and the children were amused and delighted by their ability to carry out this task.

Many children have computer programmes at home that are designed as mathematical games for leisure use and these too can help the children to realize the relevance of mathematics to their own lives.

Specific Activities Which Can Be Designed to Link Mathematics to the Real World

As well as trying to present mathematics from real-life contexts it may be helpful to draw upon the play or leisure contexts that children have met at home, such as the use of games, stories and pictures, to create a bridge between the out-of-school and in-school environments.

Games can be used in different ways to help children's mathematical understanding. First they can reinforce and consolidate skills that children already have. Second, they can help children to develop new mathematical skills and concepts. To do this effectively the games will need to be carefully planned and utilized. Teachers will need to have clear ideas of what skill or concept they are aiming to develop and monitor the playing of the games in order to assess their effectiveness. They may also need to be active in the game themselves. At the same time as encouraging learning, games, used successfully, are highly motivating to children. Ernest felt that this was the most important reason for using games in mathematics teaching.

Pupils become strongly motivated, they immerse themselves in the activity, and over a period of time should enhance their attitude towards the subject.' (Ernest, 1986: 2)

Some children enjoy playing board games at home but will often not realize that these are mathematical and require some mathematical understanding.

Suzy and Emily, for example, were playing Snakes and Ladders with Suzy's mother. They threw the dice and matched the dots on the dice to numbers one to six. They then counted out the number of spaces their counters could move along the board. They also recognized the numbers on the board that went from 0 to 50. They often called out loud the numbers that they landed on, especially when they climbed a ladder or fell down a snake!

Stories are important in children's lives. They are usually a daily part of their everyday life, including their life at school. As such they can be used as stimulation for children's learning in many areas of the curriculum, not least mathematics. An example might be using the story of 'The Three Bears' to develop children's understanding of measurement. This could be done directly by using vocabulary like 'taller' and 'heavier' or by setting up activities for the children in which they compare and sort objects for the three characters.

Sharing picture story books that allow children to count up items can be helpful too, as the children can touch their fingers as a tally or practice number order by chanting all together.

Pictures can be used in different ways to stimulate mathematical development. They are a useful resource because contemporary, up-to-date issues can be used, including pictures from newspapers. The visual stimulation is also important. As we have already seen, many children learn best through visual stimuli.

One way is to use pictures as a visual clue to help with work the children are doing. For example, if children are working out simple addition questions then relating these to actual objects pictured on a page will be a useful aid, especially if they are everyday objects such as biscuits or toy cars that the child can relate to.

 ### A Chance to Think

Tom had been working on simple subtraction problems using small 'compare' bears to help him with his counting out and taking away. He was able to write down his calculations using numbers to 20 and the subtraction and equals signs. His teacher then gave him a workbook in which to do some similar problems. Each question had an illustrated picture which he could use to help him solve the problem. So by the question '8 – 2' he saw eight cakes on a tray and then two children eating a cake each. This helped him to work out the answer as six.

Another way is to use a large picture as a focus for mathematical discussion to increase children's mathematical vocabulary. An example would be comparing the heights of buildings.

A class of 10-year-olds, for example, were grouped around a large scenic picture. This showed steep hills leading down to the sea. There were buildings dotted up the side of the hill and a small village at its base. Beneath the sea's surface could be seen a wrecked boat and marine animals. The children discussed the relative heights of the different buildings above the village and then how the depths of the wreck and creatures might be measured. The teacher used the concept of 'sea level' as a focus for discussing negative numbers.

The use of games and pictures can help children to build up images in their mind, which may help them to think about mathematical ideas. Children can be helped to expand this process by deliberate encouragement.

Imagery

Children and adults can build up pictures in their heads of mathematical ideas, mathematical models and mathematical processes. This mental modelling is known as imagery. Imagery can play a powerful part in helping children to develop secure and sophisticated mathematical understanding. Children are commonly encouraged to build up mental images of things to do with shape but imagery can be used effectively in developing all areas of the children's mathematical learning, not least number and the use of measures.

Despite the early use of imagery by some mathematicians, for many years it was a neglected area in the teaching of mathematics. As Higginson noted in 1982, too little attention had been paid 'to the role of images in mathematical understanding'.

 A Chance to Think

A brief history of the use of imagery as a mathematical learning tool. As long ago as the late nineteenth century some mathematicians were using imagery in their teaching. For example, in a lesson taught in the very early twentieth century Mary Boole used mental imagery to help her pupils understand concepts such as 'zero'. She got her pupils to close their eyes and form pictures in their minds to a series of exercises she described to them. She felt that the images they formed would help with their understanding of mathematical ideas and that such visualization could be positively helped by direct education. In one fascinating exercise she used mental images to show how a curved line is made up of many much shorter straight lines.

This is beginning to change, however. Carter (1988) explored the mental images that children construct of number lines. This built on the work of Plunkett, who several years before had also explored the importance of visual images in working with numbers. He noticed that confident mathematicians generally carried a number line in their heads, while most other people didn't. He made the important point that visual images, once made, can be permanently available and then used to aid understanding (Plunkett, 1979). More recently researchers (Pendlington, 1998, and Bills, 1999) have pointed to the importance that images can play in helping children with numeracy. For this reason it is important for teachers to understand what images children may already have and to encourage children to think about the images that they can use to aid their mathematical competence.

Resources can help children to develop the images that will support their understanding of numbers. These can include a simple number line or track, which will help them to position numbers in order, or place value cards, which show the children how to partition more complex numbers into their parts.

 A Chance to Think

Using a number track can help children to build up a mental image of the order and positioning of numbers.

Jamie was introduced to a number track that had the numbers from one to ten on it.

1	2	3	4	5	6	7	8	9	10

The teacher pointed to the numbers on the track as the children counted up to and down from ten. The number track was also displayed on the wall in the classroom and all of the children had smaller ones to use for counting. Gradually Jamie built up a picture of the numbers in his mind, which helped him to remember the order they come in, to remind him which numbers are bigger or smaller than the others and to see how they are written.

Place value cards can help the children to partition number into component parts such as the hundreds, the tens and the units.

Sara's teacher used place value cards to help her class to build up numbers in the hundreds. 657 was shown as made up of 600 + 50 + 7 as the cards were placed on top of each other. Sara worked with the cards both in building up numbers and in partitioning larger numbers into their components of hundreds, tens and units. She was in fact developing an image that showed the larger numbers being made up of the smaller numbers.

6	5	7
6	0	0
	5	0
		7

Her teacher encouraged this by giving her class specific visualization exercises. They were asked to close their eyes, think of a number in the hundreds and then describe what they saw and how the number was made up.

Teachers should think carefully about any practical apparatus they give to the children to aid mathematical computation, as it is thought that children can develop images from the materials they manipulate and then subsequently work from imagined situations (Anghileri, 2000: 10). This means that, with practice using suitable materials, children will be better able to work on mathematical problems where they do not have access to such materials. Conversely, practice with unsuitable materials, which do not demonstrate the mathematical idea clearly, can of course confuse.

The area of mathematics that springs most easily to mind when thinking about mathematical images is probably shape and space. The words that describe shapes are commonly used – 'round', 'flat' and 'square' quickly bring images to the mind. Indeed Caleb Gattegno, a well-known mathematician working in the mid-twentieth century, used to ask his university classes to engage with images as he gave them instructions. The conclusion he reached was 'that the stuff of geometry was the mental stuff called images' (Gattegno, 1965: 38). It is useful for children to have these opportunities today and games involving the identification of an orally described shape can be fun and stimulating.

 A Chance to Think

Children can enjoy imagery games especially when there is an element of competition. The children in Class 5 were sitting on the carpet, having been split into two teams. Tracey, their teacher, had a bag on her lap in which she had hidden some shapes. She chose Heather from team A to come to the front of the class, feel in the bag and describe the shape. Heather described the shape as 'a regular shape with six points [vertices], five faces and nine edges'. Team A guessed the name of the shape and were given one point. (Can you work out what it was?) Tracey then chose someone from team B to describe the next shape.

As we have said, children usually enjoy using computers and the use of computer technology has increased the opportunity for them to gain visual images of mathematical ideas. For example a LOGO program, which allows the children to construct 2D shapes, will help them to visualize not only the shapes but also the turns and angles that make them up.

Jack and Tom, for example, were working together on a LOGO program. They were trying to construct rhombi. They knew that all the sides had to be the same length. By continuous trial and error they found that in order to construct it accurately the first angle of turn and the second angle of turn had to sum to 180 degrees and that the third and fourth angles of turn had to match the first two. They then constructed a whole series of rhombi, which all had the same length sides but different internal angles. These images stayed with them and helped them to build up a real understanding of rhombi.

Materials and displays will also help younger children to form an image of different shapes. Care has to be exercised over the choice of such materials, as children who are used to seeing, for example, displays of nothing but squares, rectangles or triangles, with a horizontal base will form an image of these shapes in this plane and may not realize that the orientation of a shape is not important. This may impede their learning as they may later have difficulty recognizing these shapes when they are tilted at a different angle. Textbooks and commercially produced posters often show only regular shapes and it is a fairly common misconception among children and adults alike that hexagons, for example, are six-sided shapes with sides of the same length and angles of the same size, when in reality a hexagon is any six-sided shape. This type of misconception is caused because the right materials and visual images of irregular shapes have not been made available.

Children enjoy tasks that ask them to make mental images and can often be seen screwing their eyes up very tight and thinking hard.

In a class of 8-year-olds the teacher asked the children to close their eyes. She took them through a series of imaginary tasks:

- Picture a square, colour it as you like.
- Now take some scissors and cut off one of the corners.
- Now draw the shape you have left.
- What is it called?

Close your eyes again. Now imagine a rectangle of any colour.
- Draw a diagonal line across the shape from corner to corner and then cut along it.
- Look at the two shapes you have left and then open your eyes and draw them.

- What are they called?
- What size are their angles?
- Can they fit on each other?

This task not only asks for the shape to be imagined but also looks at symmetry and angle.

Imagery can also help children to think about measurement. Many children find this difficult, particularly when they have to use estimation skills in this area of their work. In order to estimate with some degree of accuracy you need to have a realistic image of the measure you are using (Lawrence, 1996). Being able to manipulate an image in your mind will be important in coming to a realistic estimation (Bright, 1976; Brenchley, 1986).

 ### A Chance to Think

Sam, Jo, Chelsea and Grace were working on estimating and measuring objects in metres. First their teacher gave them a series of mind exercises to do. She held up the metre stick and asked the children to look carefully at it. She then asked them to close their eyes and try to visualize the metre stick. They were then encouraged to open their eyes and compare their image with the real metre stick. The metre stick was then put away. The teacher encouraged the children to close their eyes again and imagine the metre stick. They then opened their eyes and put their imaged stick against something she wanted them to estimate, such as a blackboard or a cupboard. They wrote down their estimate before actually measuring the pieces of furniture.

Being able to estimate accurately may have been easier long ago because the names we used for our measures in the past conjured up such vivid images. For example, many of the measures used for length were those of body parts, and even today horses are still measured in 'hands'. Barleycorns measured smaller lengths and longer lengths were measured by the familiar furlong, coming from 'furrow length', a common strip of land.

In other areas of measurement too we can see that early measures would have instantly conjured up an image. We can think of the 'mouthful' used as a measure of small amounts of liquids, the 'barrel', a weight used for measuring herring, the 'load' for a volume of timber and so on. Such easily visualized measures, however, are no longer used and therefore it is more difficult for children to gain useful images. Especially confusing in this country is the still persistent informal use of, for example, stones, pounds, pints and inches.

Children can be encouraged to build up a visual image of measures by helping them to imagine usable comparisons. A group of children, for example, discussed what they imagined a centimetre to be. Sarah said that she thought it was about the length of her fingernail. She measured her nail and found it to be about one centimetre. The teacher then gave Sarah a collection of small objects to first estimate and then measure in centimetres. The teacher told her to think of how many images of her fingernail she could fit alongside each object before giving her estimate. Sarah said that she felt much more confident in giving her estimates, which were no longer blind guesses.

Clayton (1988) found that children made less successful estimates with metric units than with imperial units. The use of imperial units is diminishing but many parents and grandparents still think in and talk to the children in these terms. Supermarket shopping too means that today everything is either pre-packaged or you are expected to serve yourself and so there is no longer any need to ask for a particular weight of fruit, vegetables or meat. When you do need to stipulate a quantity, you can usually get away with saying how many slices you want or agreeing an amount when a shop assistant demonstrates and asks 'This much?' Children therefore do not have the practical experience that they once had and in school they often make rather wild estimates, which are in fact guesses only. However, practical imagery exercises can help children to hone their measurement estimation skills.

 ### A Chance to Think

Ben, Mary and Mark were estimating the capacity of a variety of bottles and plastic boxes in litres and half litres. Their teacher asked them what a litre measure was and Ben said that his Mum bought orange juice in litre cartons. The other children agreed with Ben. They were familiar with the kind of carton the orange juice came in. Their teacher encouraged them to close their eyes and imagine a carton of orange. They then opened their eyes and she held up one of the bottles that needed to be estimated. She asked them to imagine how many cartons of orange would fit into the bottle. They then made their estimates and checked them by filling up the bottle with water.

Building of images to help children with their mathematical development relies to some extent on mathematical modelling. In Japan children are encouraged to model and explain their mathematical thinking to others.

Mathematics and Problem-solving – the Japanese Example

Like children in the Netherlands, Japanese children have also consistently performed well in international comparisons of mathematical ability. They performed particularly well in number and algebra and their performance showed them to be nearly one and a half years in advance of English pupils when measured by these tests alone. There is also less of a gap in Japan between the performance of the most able pupils and the least able children.

Perhaps one reason for the success of Japanese teaching and learning in mathematics is the emphasis that is put upon the children's explaining their reasoning. Although the curriculum for primary-age children is narrower than that in many other countries, particularly in the first years of schooling, from the beginning the children are expected to discuss and think about the mathematics with which they are engaging.

 A Chance to Think

Whitburn (2000) describes a class of 6-year-olds in Japan. Each child was given 17 cubes. For most of the lesson they discussed the different ways in which these could be arranged and what they thought the best arrangement would be. By the end of the lesson they had decided the most convenient way to group the cubes was in a ten and a seven (Whitburn, 2000). The activity helped them to develop a strong understanding of place value.

As Japanese children grow older, many of their lessons relate to a central problem posed by the teacher. The children are expected to work on the problem either individually or in groups and this is followed by whole-class discussion as different children model their findings for the rest of the class. A similar pattern is followed with homework. The children are given a problem and then share their answers the next day with the rest of their class, explaining their thought processes.

A class of 9-year-olds was asked 'How large is the classroom?' The whole class discussed how this might be measured. They talked about the comparison of length and width and this led on to discussion of area measurement and both square centimetres and square metres. Then, working in groups, they began to grasp the relationship between length, width and area. They then calculated the length, width and area of the classroom and considered other area measurements.

Emphasis in Japan seems to be on the mathematical processes that the children work out and develop for themselves and their ability to model and explain their mathematical ideas. Knowledge content has lower priority than the development of the children's mathematical thinking. This notion takes us neatly back to Nunes and Bryant's assertion, already cited in Chapter 1, that if children understand how mathematical knowledge is constructed then they can generate knowledge that they have not learned directly for themselves (Nunes and Bryant, 1996).

Summary

In this chapter we have discussed the way in which mathematical skills are useful to everyone, including children. This fact is not always appreciated and sometimes people do not realize the extent to which they engage in mathematics in their everyday lives. This suggests, therefore, that it is important to provide pupils with learning environments that are stimulating and interesting to them as this will help them to develop mathematically by giving the subject personal relevance and meaning.

Mathematics in real life is most often used to solve problems so it is important that there is an emphasis on this within the mathematics that is taught in school. Making sure that these problem-solving scenarios are based on realistic contexts, as they do in the Netherlands, probably gives children the best opportunity to become fluent in using mathematical skills and procedures. Realistic contexts can be provided for the children by using the environment as a stimulus for mathematical work. In addition, making sure that mathematics permeates and is permeated by other areas of learning ensures that mathematics is not perceived as a tricky, separate subject that has to be learned in isolation. Cross-curricular, integrated work can also help pupils to relate the mathematics that they do in school to their everyday experiences.

Children's natural interest and enthusiasm can be captured by relating their mathematics work to their familiar and favoured leisure pursuits, which might include the use of story, the media and computers. Work related to familiar activity can also help to create a bridge between children's out-of-school mathematics and their school mathematics.

Finally, encouraging the children to build up mathematical images and the ability to model and explain mathematical ideas may be important in developing confident and competent mathematicians of the future.

Reflective Questions

- In what ways can you make mathematics meaningful for the children in your class?
- Will lessons from abroad affect your teaching? If so, in what ways?
- How might you integrate mathematics into the rest of the curriculum?
- Think of three circumstances in which you could use imagery to help children to develop mathematical concepts.

REFERENCES AND FURTHER READING

Anghileri, J. (2000) *Teaching Number Sense*, London: Continuum.

Atkinson, S. (1995) *Mathematics with Reason*, London: Hodder and Stoughton.

Bills, L. (1999) 'What was in your head when you were thinking of that?', *Mathematics Teaching*, 168.

Boole, M. (1972) 'A lesson on curves', in Tahta, D. (ed.) *A Boolean Anthology*, London: ATM.

Brenchley, M. (1986) 'The scales of my mind, an investigation into the process of estimation with regard to measurement in young children', unpublished thesis B.Ed (Hons), Reading University.

Bright, G .W. (1976) 'Estimation as part of learning to measure', in Nelson, D. and Reys, R. (eds) *Measurement in School Mathematics*, 1976 School Yearbook, Reston, VA: NCTM.

Carter, B. (1988) 'Number Lines', in Chatley J. *Readings in Mathematical Education: Mathematical Images*, London: ATM.

Clayton, J. (1988) 'Estimation in schools', *The British Society for Research into Learning Mathematics: Proceedings from a Conference at Warwick University, May 1988*.

Coles, D. and Copeland, T. (2002) *Numeracy and Mathematics across the Primary Curriculum*, London: Fulton.

DfEE (1999) *National Numeracy Strategy*.

Ernest, P. (1986) 'Games: a rationale for their use in the teaching of mathematics in school', *Mathematics in School*, January.

Gattegno, C. (1965) 'Mathematics and imagery', *Mathematics Teacher*, 77, 515–17.

Heuvel-Panhuizen, M. (2001), 'Realistic mathematics education in the Netherlands', in Anghileri J. (ed.) *Principles and Practices in Arithmetic Teaching*, Buckingham: Open University Press.

Higginson, W. (1982) 'Symbols, icons and mathematical understanding', *Visible Language*, XVI (3), 239–48.

Lange, J. (2003) www.freudenthal.nl.

Lawrence, C. (1996) 'Imagery and Estimation', unpublished M.Phil, Milton Keynes: Open University.

Nunes, T. and Bryant, P. (1996) *Children Doing Mathematics*, London: Blackwell.

Passey, D., Rogers, C., Machell, J. and McHugh, G. (2004) *The Motivational Effect of ICT on Pupils*, DfEE research report RR523.

Pendlington, S. (1998) 'Primary children's imagery in arithmetic', *Mathematics Teaching*, British Society for Research into Learning Mathematics.

Plunkett, S. (1979) 'Icons', *Mathematics Teaching*, 103.

Treffers, A. and Beishuizen, J.J. (1999) 'Realistic mathematics education in the Netherlands', in Thompson, I. (ed.) *Issues in Teaching Numeracy in Primary Schools*, Buckingham: Open University Press.

Whitburn, J. (2000) *Strength in Numbers*, Whitstable: National Institute of Economic and Social Research.

Teaching and Learning Mathematics

INTRODUCTION

In the first two chapters we looked at current research and how that might impinge on the way that mathematics is taught within the primary school and in pre-school settings. In this chapter and the ones that follow, we will look, on a more practical level, at how our understanding of the nature of mathematics, the influences that impinge on children's learning from outside school and international research might shape the way in which mathematics is taught and learned within school and pre-school.

'Effectiveness' is currently a watchword in the teaching community. Many hours are spent each year in pursuit of greater effectiveness in teaching and learning, either as a result of professional pride, which seeks constantly to improve performance, or because of external demands, for example, school governors, Local Education Authorities, baseline and other assessments or inspectors. This applies to all curriculum areas and across both pre-school settings and schools. Within mathematics the drive is no less evident. In order to pursue the goal of 'effective mathematics teaching' it is necessary for the classroom teacher and pre-school practitioner to consider how interaction between the pupils, the teacher and other adults in the classroom as well as with the mathematics might be facilitated.

This chapter will therefore look at:

- Pupil and teacher interaction
- Providing a context
- Making connections within mathematics
- Effective questioning
- Mathematical modelling
- Recognizing and using misconceptions
- Using ICT to enhance teaching and learning within the classroom

We will concentrate particularly on the ways in which effective teaching can enhance mathematics learning and explore the ways in which teachers and practitioners can make the most of the learning situation for the children. In this chapter the word 'teacher' is used to describe anyone who 'teaches' the children; this may be the class teacher, a classroom assistant, a teaching assistant, a nursery nurse or an early-years practitioner.

Pupil and Teacher Interaction

Excellent pupil–teacher and pupil–pupil interaction is crucial as we seek to become more effective in the teaching of mathematics.

A paper written by Askew, Brown, Rhodes, Wiliam and Johnson (1997) highlighted the importance of the exchange of ideas and cited effective interaction as one of the basic means of securing children's understanding.

The primary belief here is that teaching mathematics is based on dialogue between teacher and pupils and pupils and pupils to explore each other's understandings. (Askew et al., *1997: 343)*

The ideal is to have a classroom atmosphere that is characterized by a lively mix of discussion, questioning, debate and reasoning related to the mathematics under consideration. This environment will be one where the children respond well to the prompting and questioning of the teacher. Equally this environment will be one where the teacher responds well to the children in terms of encouragement and recognition of the ideas that they present and the suggestions that they make. There are several characteristics that are usually present wherever there is good pupil–teacher interaction: clear expectations on the teacher's and pupils' part; positive and supportive relationships with the children; the appropriate amount of challenge; and positive attitudes towards mathematics leading to the children's engagement and enjoyment.

Teachers need to have clear and realistic expectations of the children's responses to their mathematical teaching, as this is central to developing good interaction in the classroom. Children need to know that they are expected to try hard, join in and make suggestions. In order to feel comfortable with this, children need to understand that their suggestions will be taken seriously and that points raised are for discussion. They also need to know that making a mistake is acceptable and others will not criticize or humiliate them if or when this happens

The teacher's relationship with the children is the most important element in securing effective interaction not only between teacher and pupils but also between pupils and pupils. There are as many different styles of working within the classroom as there are teachers, but all successful classrooms are characterized by a positive working relationship between the children and their teacher.

Positive attitudes and a non-threatening atmosphere meant that the children in the following class were happy to talk to each other about their mathematical thinking.

A class of Year 2 children were asked mental mathematics questions by their teacher.

Teacher   Can anyone add 41 and 39?

James   I can, it's 82.

Teacher   How did you come to that number, James?

James   I know that they are both near to forty so I took off 1 from the 41 to make 40 and added 1 to the 39 to make 40 and then I doubled them. I had 2 left, so I added them on.

Yasmin   But that's not right. The answer is 80.

James   But they are near doubles and I doubled 40 and I had 2 over.

Yasmin   Yes, you did that bit [adding 40] right and you had 2 over, but one was a take away and one was an add, so if you add 1 and take 1 away then that is zero, so you don't add any on.

James   I don't understand what you mean.

Teacher   You did very well, James, and a good way to tackle the question was to double 40. You just added both of the 1s at the end, which gave you the wrong final answer. Can you show us how you dealt with the 1s, by writing it on the whiteboard, Yasmin, please.

Yasmin wrote her solution on the board and James could see where he had made a mistake. The children in this class were happy to discuss their mathematics with each other because the teacher had created a supportive atmosphere in which children were willing and confident enough to make and discuss mistakes.

Children thrive upon an element of challenge in their work. It is essential that the level of challenge, however small or great, is appropriate and spurs the child on to achieve, rather than intimidates or demotivates.

If teachers model a positive view of mathematics and act as advocates for mathematics, then the children are more likely to view mathematics in a positive light. As we have seen, many adults have a negative view of mathematics: 'I can't do it', 'It's too hard!' or 'I was never any good at maths'. Teachers' positive attitudes may help to counteract any negativity from home and develop the conditions where children's motivation and confidence can be raised to ensure high-quality pupil–teacher and pupil–pupil interaction.

What is presented to children in the classroom will determine how effectively they can engage with the mathematics.

 A Chance to Think

A word of caution!
Denvir and Askew (2001: 30) believe that while children can often be seen to be participating in mathematics lessons, that in itself does not necessarily mean that they are engaging with the mathematical thinking. Teachers need to be aware that sometimes there is a strong 'performative' element to classroom discussion, which prompts children to adopt participating behaviours that have little to do with actual learning.

One of the by-products of well-planned, high-quality pupil–teacher and pupil–pupil interaction is that the process of learning becomes more enjoyable. Conversely, if the children are enjoying the lesson then the quality of interaction is likely to be higher.

A small study on exchanges of dialogue in a numeracy lesson was carried out by an undergraduate student, looking at the interaction between 9-year-old children and their teacher. The student undertook an observation in each of two classes.

The two interaction tracking sheets that she compiled looked like this.

Tracking sheet – class 1

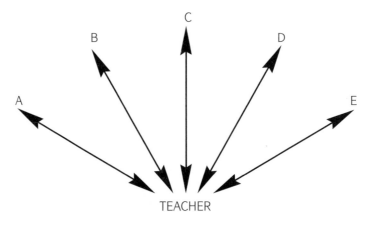

Tracking sheet – class 2

What do these diagrams tell you about the teaching styles of these two teachers?

Providing a Context

The teacher's choice of materials, contexts and approaches need to be well matched to the children to ensure that they are interested and motivated and therefore fully engaged with the mathematics.

Setting a context in which children can learn mathematics is important as it allows them to develop an understanding of the structure of mathematical knowledge so that they can apply it in new situations (already discussed in Chapters 1 and 2). This is not necessarily an easy task, especially when teachers feel constrained by what they think is expected in terms of curriculum delivery. Nevertheless, as the contexts within which mathematics is learned seem so important to the outcomes, teachers should try to give as much thought to them when planning the children's learning as they can.

In particular, teachers need to think about whether there is already a specific context in which the mathematics is set and, if not, then think about a context in which the mathematical topic could be explored, which would interest and challenge the children. It is also necessary to think about whether the children can relate to the context that you are planning to use – whether it is within their experience, whether they will enjoy it and whether it is realistic and has the potential to enhance children's learning.

A group of 8-year-old children wanted to contribute to an appeal for their local children's hospice. Their teacher saw the possibilities here to look at profit and loss. She allowed the children a sum of money to begin with, which she explained would have to be returned at the end of the project. The children set about working out how they might make the best return on the money that they had been given. Other groups of children joined in the fundraising, which became a competition to see who could raise the biggest percentage profit on the starting fund.

Making Connections within Mathematics

Askew *et al.* (1997) identified three approaches to the teaching of mathematics to children. They are the transmission model, the connectionist model and the discovery model. Askew *et al.* highlighted the importance of using a connectionist approach to mathematics teaching and learning, in which specific links are made between areas of mathematics. He believed that this approach is more effective than either transmission, where the teacher gives the children the information they need to complete a task, or discovery, where the teacher provides the mathematical resources and environment and the children discover their own methods of tackling mathematical problems. Facilitating the making of connections within mathematics and between mathematics and other areas of learning is crucial to the development of the broad mathematical understanding that we desire for the children. This connectionist approach affects several areas of our mathematics teaching. We need to consider not only the connections between mathematical concepts but also connections between mathematical responses and language, mathematical symbols, images and diagrams.

Helping children to see all these connections increases their ability to view mathematics as a cohesive entity, rather than just a series of unconnected facts that need to be learned. As the connections between different mathematical ideas are made clear, so the children develop a greater awareness of how understanding of one area can aid their understanding of another area.

Making connections does not usually happen by accident and many children do not see the connections for themselves; they need to be made explicit. It is therefore incumbent upon the teacher to plan to highlight these connections. If we agree with social constructivists such as Vygotsky (1978) and Bruner (1986), who advocate that the most effective teaching occurs when the children start from a known knowledge base and then build on this through interaction with a more knowledgeable other, then planning to develop these connections directly will enhance both the effectiveness of our teaching and the children's learning.

The vast array of possible connections within mathematics makes it impossible to list them all here. However, some of the more obvious and important connections related to number are listed below:

- Subtraction (inverse of addition)
- Addition (inverse of subtraction)
- Multiplication (repeated addition)
- Multiplication (connection between different times tables)
- Division (repeated subtraction)
- Division (link with times tables)
- Vulgar fractions (percentages, decimals, ratios, proportion)
- Decimals (vulgar fractions, percentages, ratios, proportion, measures)
- Ratio (percentages, decimals, proportion)
- Percentages (decimals, ratios, proportion)
- Interconnection between vulgar fractions
- Vulgar fractions (links with times tables)

As well as connections between mathematical concepts there are also connections to be made between mathematical ideas and mathematical language.

The language that is associated with mathematics is often specific and very precise. As children get to grips with mathematical ideas, so they encounter an increasing mathematical vocabulary. In order for the children to build upon their current experience this vocabulary must be taught, modelled and used naturally in learning contexts. Children need to develop familiarity and be at ease with using the correct mathematical terms when engaged in their work. This is not just so that they may appear intelligent (especially to parents, who often would not expect an 8-year-old to discuss the different factors of 24!), but because of the nature of mathematics itself. There is a precision inherent in mathematical language that is essential to understanding the mathematics itself.

The English National Numeracy Strategy 'Mathematical Vocabulary' booklet (2000: 1) states that

Mathematical language is crucial to the children's development of thinking. If children don't have the vocabulary to talk about division, or perimeters, or numerical difference, they cannot make progress in understanding these areas of knowledge.

Use of appropriate mathematical language separates and isolates mathematical ideas to communicate a clear picture of the situation being described. For many mathematicians, there is a beauty and clarity in the use of such language. For the children we teach, it is essential that they make the necessary connection between the language and the mathematical situation needing description. As well as the teacher modelling the necessary mathematical language it is also important that the children use mathematical words themselves, by working in groups with other children and by getting the opportunity to explain their mathematical ideas to the teacher and the rest of the class.

It has been suggested that mathematical words can be put into three categories (Shuard and Rothery, 1984). There are those words that are in use in everyday life for non-mathematical purposes but which in mathematics have different and precise meanings such as 'units' (kitchen), 'take away' (Chinese) or 'table' (something you eat from). These words can confuse children and easily cause misunderstanding. Then there are words that have a similar but less precise meaning in everyday life, such as 'reflection' and 'divide' which can sometimes confuse but conversely can sometimes help the children, as they are close in meaning to the mathematical term and give children a clue as to the mathematical meaning. Third, there are technical words such as 'circle', 'ratio' and 'multiply', which often describe complex mathematical ideas and can only be applied mathematically. They have to be learned within the context of mathematics and are often difficult to explain, understand and remember.

Children often find it hard to learn how to use mathematical symbols. As they struggle to develop their writing and language skills they are suddenly expected to recognize that when working with mathematical situations certain (seemingly random) squiggles have a specific meaning. Yet it is essential that children gradually develop an understanding of these symbols and their use.

 A Chance to Think

A group of 7-year-old children were making up sentences about some chocolate frogs provided by the teacher. The children then converted these into number sentences. A written sentence might read

I have 17 chocolate frogs. Harry gives me 9 more. I have 26 chocolate frogs altogether.

Change this to a number sentence and it reads

17 frogs + 9 more = 26 frogs

The practice of integrating mathematical symbols into their sentences helped the children to start making the connection between the symbols and the language being used.

It is a mistake to ask the children to use mathematical symbols very early in their experience. Mathematical symbols are a highly abstract way of communication. There is also the additional complication that mathematical symbols are associated with numerous mathematical words. Children need time to become familiar with these symbols and comfortable in using them with the extensive mathematical vocabulary that is associated with them. For effective learning to take place these issues must be addressed and planned for. One way of doing this is to have flash cards containing the symbols which can be shown to the children alongside the mathematical word or words that they represent.

Some examples of mathematical symbols and their meanings:

Symbol	Associated language
+	Add, plus, more than, increase, larger than, sum, total, etc.
−	Subtract, minus, less than, difference, smaller than, etc.
×	Multiplied by, times, groups of, lots of, sets of, etc.
÷	Divided by, split into groups, etc.

As discussed in Chapter 2, images form an important part of teaching mathematical ideas. For many children the ability to make sense of an image is crucial to their development of a particular mathematical concept. It is vital that the teacher is able to ensure that suitable images, whether apparatus or pictures, are provided that enable the correct connections to be made between the image and the mathematical concept. For example, the provision of a number track, rather than a number line, when dealing with parts of whole numbers such as decimals or fractions can be confusing for the child.

Some sources of mathematical images might be:
Pictorial representation of something
- Picture
- Photograph
- Graph

An image of a physical object
- 3D shape
- Measuring cylinder
- Measuring scale

An image of a numerical process
- Addition on a number line
- Multiplication array
- Fractions

As with all areas of mathematics that teachers wish to develop, opportunities to develop mental images need to be planned for carefully, but teachers also need to be alert to instances that arise, in the natural course of events, in which images can be used to support the children's learning. Opportunities must be seized and the connections clearly established to enable learning to be further secured.

Similarly pupils need to understand the mathematical connections in mathematical diagrams. Such diagrams can aid children who learn most effectively in a visual manner. Seeing how something works in a diagrammatic context gives the children the visual 'hooks' on which to hang their understanding. In the world outside school mathematical diagrams are utilized by the media to describe many situations and children need to develop an understanding of these charts and diagrams in order to make an informed decision about their meaning.

Some of the diagrams that children need to become familiar with include graphical representation such as block graphs, bar charts and pie charts. Others include Venn, Carroll and tree diagrams.

1. Bar chart

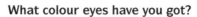

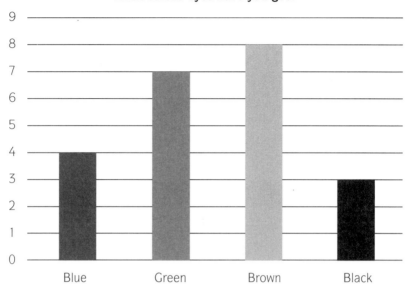

2. As a Pie chart

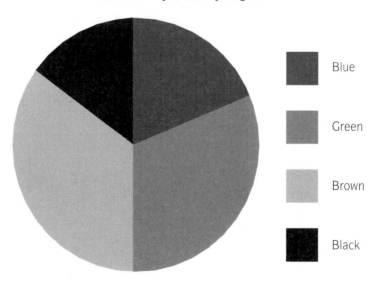

3. Venn diagram

Sort the coloured shapes

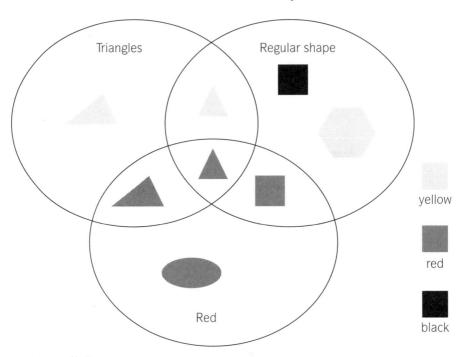

4. A Carroll diagram

Sort the coloured shapes

	triangle	not triangle
red		
not red		

yellow

red

black

5. A tree diagram

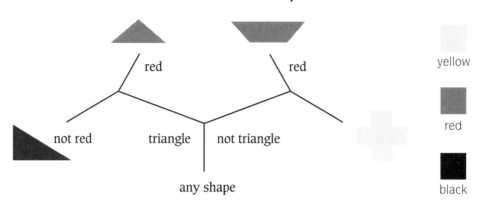

Sort the coloured shapes

red

red

yellow

not red

triangle | not triangle

red

any shape

black

Discussing charts and graphs found in the newspaper or on the Internet can give children a real insight into the uses of these data presentation forms and offer a means of effective questioning.

Effective Questioning

Effective questioning can help to close the gap between what the children already understand and what they need to learn. Questions that are initiated by the teacher are useful for finding out what children know and understand and in a supportive environment child-initiated questions can bring about a negotiated and shared understanding of a mathematical problem or idea and give pupils some control over their own learning (Baumfield and Mroz, 2002). Effective questioning is the heartbeat of a stimulating learning environment.

Some of the opportunities that effective questioning can provide are:

- Appropriate challenge for children's individual needs
- Encouragement for the children
- Assessment
- Creating an inclusive atmosphere
- Prompting higher-order thinking skills
- Creating a real interaction between the pupils and the ideas that are being taught
- Allowing the children to explore mathematical questions
- Allowing children to seek clarification

- Discussion with one another and the teacher
- Control of their own learning
- A range of responses to be considered by the whole class or group

Effective questioning is dependent upon a well-judged blend of open, closed and leading questions. As the teacher develops greater expertise, so the questions are woven into a web that is skilfully designed to capture the concept being taught within the child's understanding. Some of these questions will require a direct answer from the child, but as the teacher becomes more confident some questions will allow the children to discuss mathematical ideas with both the teacher and each other. Good questioning will also allow the children to ask questions both of the teacher and of each other. This complex web of questions, answers and counter-questions will allow the children to develop a greater understanding of the mathematical concept under discussion. Knowing when to use an open or a closed question, as well as judging at what point to introduce a leading question comes with practice and with knowing the children.

 A Chance to Think

Here are some examples of open and closed questions. Which of these do you think could encourage discussion between the children?

Open questions	Good for ...
Which numbers added together can make 10?	Assessing a broad understanding
How did you work out your answer?	Developing strategies
Why do you think a square can also be called a rectangle?	Developing a child's use of specific mathematical language
What do you know about pentagons and tessellation?	Developing higher-order thinking skills
Closed questions	**Good for ...**
What is the product of 3 and 5?	Assessing specific knowledge
James, what is the square root of 144?	Assessing specific under-standing of a particular child
Addition is the inverse of what?	Focusing the children upon specific mathematical information

Leading questions	Good for ...
An equilateral triangle has angles of 60°, so the angles inside a triangle add up to ...?	Acting as an aide-mémoire
All quadrilaterals have four sides. How many sides does a square have? What type of shape is a square?	Helping children to establish links between ideas

What is most important is that teachers evaluate their own questioning styles. Many will find that open-ended questions predominate. Others will find that closed questions do. For yet others, questions are characteristically leading questions. Once you have analysed your own style, you should practise using the questioning techniques that do not feature as prominently as others. This will then make your questioning strategy more comprehensive, which in turn should increase your effectiveness and the quality of the children's learning.

Mathematical Modelling

Another tool that many teachers use to enhance their effectiveness within the classroom is that of modelling mathematics.

In mathematical modelling a teacher or pupil demonstrates, or 'models', a particular idea to learners. In many instances teachers model processes, sequences and explanations to the children. In many other instances children model their own explanations, along with the processes and procedures used, to their classmates. Usually these opportunities are accompanied by a great deal of discussion with the children, along with specific, targeted questioning from the class teacher to ensure understanding. It is a fundamentally interactive element of the teaching process, not just an opportunity for 'chalk and talk', with a passive audience listening in. Modelling is focused sharply upon the issue under consideration and the teacher must ensure contributions are pertinent to the issue. This type of mathematical modelling features strongly in the way Japanese children are taught mathematics (see Chapter 2 for more discussion on this).

Mathematical modelling by the teacher does not have to be saved for complex mathematical processes and ideas. Indeed, in the Stepping Stones section of the English Foundation Stage Curriculum Guidance practitioners are recommended to 'model and encourage the use of mathematical language such as "count", "count on", "how many", "altogether", "add", "one less" and "the number before"' and to 'pose more complex problems, for example sharing a number of things when there will be a remainder' (DfES, 2000: 77).

The benefits of modelling may be slightly different depending upon whether it is teacher or pupil doing the modelling. Modelling by the teacher ensures that the children are focused on the precise process that the teacher wants, allows for accurate mathematical language to be used in the right context and ensures discussion. When the children are sharing their ideas with others by modelling mathematical processes it is likely that the other children will be able to relate more easily to the language and logical structures involved. It also ensures that the children understand how much their work is valued, which in turn promotes a positive perception of themselves as mathematicians. Finally it gives the children an opportunity to use the correct mathematical language associated with the mathematics that they are modelling.

Modelling a particular mathematical skill or concept, either for children or by children, actively promotes interactive learning, that is, it enables children to learn from each other or from the teacher. It can also help to pick up and deal with or prevent misconceptions or can be used in response to misconceptions. Inviting children to explain how the teacher or the pupil arrived at the answer or asking why a problem was approached in a particular way encourages children to think things through, thus prompting higher-order mathematical thinking skills (McGuinness, 1999).

Misconceptions: Recognizing and Using Them

Successful teachers have always recognized and addressed misconceptions within children's work. It is a natural progression from monitoring and marking. It is an integral element within any discussion with a child or a class of children. Askew and Wiliam (1995) believe that: 'Learning is more effective when common misconceptions are addressed, exposed and discussed in teaching.'

Much educational research has been undertaken into this area, particularly in evaluating the precise nature of the misconceptions in almost all areas of mathematical understanding. Understanding how certain misconceptions arise can make a valuable contribution to teaching and consequently to children's learning. It is not the intention of this book, however, to delve into the reasons why some children misunderstand an element of place value, for example; rather, it is to point the way to using this research in the classroom.

Several authors have identified the various sources of misconception, which can be summarized as follows (see Koshy, 2000: 175)

Errors due to an accidental mistake (adding 3 + 4 = 8)
- Boredom (the mathematics is not stimulating the children)
- Distraction (often related to friends, football or TV!)
- Carelessness ('I need to finish these to get out to play on time.')
- Lack of practice (Beware! Although more practice can be the right solution, too often it only makes children practise their misunderstanding, thus reinforcing it, rather than allowing them to see the causes of the inaccuracy.)

Errors due to a reliance on rules
- Lack of understanding of a rule
- Application of a rule in an inappropriate context
- Only partial application of a rule
- Faulty procedure or 'Bug' (Thompson, 1999: 169; Askew, 1998: 91 ff.)
- Invented rules' (Askew,1998: 92) e.g. adding a zero to multiply by ten
- 'False rules' (Askew,1998: 92), e.g. multiplying always makes numbers bigger

Errors due to a misunderstanding of the vocabulary used
- I thought subtraction meant 'times'
- I didn't know what sum meant

Errors due to lack of conceptual understanding
- Multiplying always makes the number larger

Once a problem with a child's work has been identified the next step is to decide how best to proceed. The teacher has various options, for example to correct the mistake and carry on as if it had not been made, to have an in-depth discussion with the child about the nature of the mistake or to stop the whole class and discuss the issue as a whole-class teaching point.

Each of these strategies has its merits. Sometimes it is clear that a child has just made a simple error in calculation, which on most other occasions would not occur. If the teacher knows the class well, he or she will recognize this and a simple correction will be appropriate. Sometimes the error is more profound and warrants a more comprehensive and detailed discussion with the child. Whether to make this misconception public will depend on the child involved and whether the teacher knows, from continuous assessment, that the misconception is common to other children in the class.

 ### *A Chance to Think*

Carl, aged 10, was asked
'What is the product of 6 and 3?' He answered '9.'
Because Carl (and other children in the class) appeared to have a problem with this particular mathematical language, the teacher initiated a discussion about what 'product' meant.
James and Fatima, who had not made this mistake, modelled how they had arrived at their answers. Using the correct mathematical language they explained their methods and the underlying concepts.
Carl went on to answer another 'product' question correctly, demonstrating that he now understood the meaning of the word product and the mathematical process that he needed to employ in order to find it. His misunderstanding had been corrected.

There are also occasions when it is clear that the misconception is limited to perhaps one or two children only. In this instance it is most effective if discussions take place on an individual (or a small group) basis. When working with a small group it is possible to establish the source of the misconception clearly and plan steps to correct it. The teacher should not just explain but should interact with the children so that they are actively involved and engaged in the mathematics. Telling the child how to get the answer is a short-term solution and it is almost guaranteed that the child will forget how to do it before the next lesson, if not earlier.

When dealing with misconceptions there are several key features that should be remembered.

Key feature	Implication
Unattainable perfection	No matter what you do children will develop misunderstandings
Diagnosis	Teachers must get to the root of the misconception to ensure effective action to secure understanding
Key feature	**Implication**
Planning with misconceptions in mind	Recognize where misconceptions may arise and plan to deal with them
Don't just re-teach (do it again)	Approach the idea from a different angle Try using different materials, or resources or frame within a different context Modelling processes (by children and teacher) is important
Cater for different learning styles	Recognize that children learn in different ways and cater for this

As we have seen, the potential for effective teaching as misconceptions arise is significant. However, 'most children do not perceive mistakes as having any positive effect on their learning' (Koshy, 2000: 173) and many children view any form of error as a wholly negative experience. So teachers need to create a positive and sensitive classroom in which children view learning from misconceptions as part of normal practice and where no stigma is attached to the need to tackle errors. Developing this classroom ethos allows the most effective use to be made of the opportunities afforded from diagnosing misconceptions. Better still is when this ethos is school policy and continuity of approach from class to class and key stage to key stage is maintained. There is more about managing misconceptions in Chapter 5.

Using ICT to Enhance Teaching and Learning Within the Classroom

Many teachers would agree that using ICT within the classroom has the potential to enhance the quality of the children's mathematical learning, but always clear focus should be upon enhancing pupils' learning, rather than on the technology itself. Obviously the specification of the equipment needs to be appropriate for the task, but this is for the ICT coordinator to manage. In the same way, the children need to have the skills necessary to access any computer program that is being considered for use, but these skills should be developed within ICT-specific sessions. In using ICT to teach mathematics, the focus should be exclusively on the mathematics.

So, for example, if a class of children were investigating number patterns within the context of multiplication, the children could use Excel and the 'drag and fill' technique and could then investigate the patterns using the spreadsheet. Familiarity with these ICT skills would enable the children to concentrate on the mathematical elements of the task, looking for the patterns, hypothesizing, predicating, developing reasoning skills, developing mathematical vocabulary and so on.

Naturally, you need to consider how appropriate it is to use ICT at all. ICT should be used if it is an effective resource to enable the children to develop their skills and understanding. However, if ICT is not the most effective resource then it should not be used. The sole criterion is whether ICT helps to develop the understanding of the children.

 A Chance to Think

Consider these two examples. Which one do you think illustrates the effective use of ICT?

Example 1
Year 6 children Djamila and Deji were investigating number sequences. They had a good understanding of how to use the computer program Excel (including entering and using simple formulae) and had identified a possible pattern to the sequence they were investigating. They wanted to test whether this pattern would work for other numbers in the sequence and wanted to use Excel to test their ideas. They were able to use the spreadsheet. They entered the formula, tested their predictions and were able to create a graph to demonstrate their success in identifying the pattern. In addition, it enabled them to identify the nth term.

Example 2
Year 3 pupils Levi and Krystal had surveyed their class to find out which pop group was their favourite. They had completed the unit of work that had developed their understanding of bar charts. The information had been displayed effectively in the classroom using hand-drawn graphs. They understood how to draw simple charts using

software called Number Magic. Their teacher asked them to transfer the results of their survey on to Number Magic to create another version of their bar chart.

There can be some significant benefits from using ICT. Many children, for example, are more actively engaged when using ICT, it often allows more interactive engagement and in certain contexts it gives children the opportunity to model solutions. Furthermore, it can be particularly beneficial to those children whose learning style is more visual. It can also, to some extent, help to bridge the home–school gap as many children have a computer at home, which they can use for leisure activity such as game playing.

What sorts of opportunities are available for the children to use ICT in mathematics?

Type of ICT	Pro	Con
Adapting programs to develop mathematical ideas (e.g. spreadsheets)	Allows teacher to adapt software to pupil needs Flexible	Children need to have prior knowledge of the program
Interactive teaching programs (e.g. those available on the www.standards.dfes.gov.uk website such as measuring a cylinder)	Easily available. Portable (fit on a floppy disk). Simple	Instructions are not that clear (practice before using in class)
Individualized learning programs (e.g. RM Learning System)	Allows children to work at own pace Children enjoy using it Flexibility (can be organized to suit class/school) Allows specific children to be targeted for frequent input Clear feedback on progress	Does not mirror taught sessions in class Does not allow for discussion with peers Cannot replace class teaching (should only be used in conjunction with it) Expensive
Mathematics-based programs (e.g. Mighty Maths Challenge)	Often in games format which children enjoy Some games allow for problem-solving	Often 'drill and practice' format that does not extend children

Type of ICT	Pro	Con
Calculators	Easy to use OHT version is very useful Cheap	
Floor turtles	Excellent to develop children's understanding of several areas of shape and space Good for developing mathematical discussion	Quite costly Storage space required Several needed for a whole-class activity

ICT is an area that is growing rapidly and overhead projectors, data projectors and interactive whiteboards are now seen in many schools. Used well, ICT can provide increased interactivity and participation, allowing the children to become more engaged with their learning, which reinforces the skills and understanding being developed. ICT can also enable lessons to be delivered at a pace that matches the needs of the children and visual learners may benefit from the visual stimuli.

All teachers must exercise an informed judgement about the use of ICT as a teaching tool. A key question to ask is 'What is the best way to teach this aspect of mathematics?' Sometimes ICT will be beneficial, sometimes not.

Although ICT obviously has some important benefits to offer, it goes without saying that using ICT does not guarantee successful teaching and learning. The most important element in the process is still the class teacher. A lesson will still lack interactivity or pace despite the use of ICT if the teacher does not create these.

There are two key elements in ICT resources: software and hardware.

There are too many software programs that can be used effectively in the classroom to list here. What is important is to consider the advantages and disadvantages of the software available in the school. If you or the children, for example, are using a custom-built piece of software to demonstrate number bonds, but it takes you five minutes to create the example that you want to show the children, then it is likely to reduce rather than increase your effectiveness as a teacher. However, if the class teacher and the children use a desktop publishing package to create their own examples of number bonds and to explain their workings out, this is a more effective use of software. There is no magic list; what works for you and your class is the most important consideration.

The Internet is not technically a piece of software, but it does provide a portal to a huge range of resources, some of which is software. Conversely some web-based resources can be little more than online worksheets with great potential for inappropriate use as drill and practice sheets. Teachers need to take some time to investigate thoroughly various websites to ensure that they access the best materials to use with their children. There are some excellent interactive teaching programs available on the Internet, such as the 'What's my angle?' software on www.standards.dfes.gov/numeracy.

Unfortunately teachers often equate hardware with the ubiquitous PC. The scope of ICT goes far beyond this and it is important to remember that, as well as interactive smart boards, laptops and data projectors, other elements should also be taken into consideration, such as calculators, tape recorders, video cameras, digital cameras and so on.

The ICT suite is a prominent feature in many schools and while it has the potential to make a significant positive impact upon children's learning, it can also limit their progress. There is undoubtedly much good practice in using ICT suites to develop the ICT skills of children, but this is not always the case when the focus of the teaching is another subject, such as mathematics. There may be a timetabling issue: 'We only get one session per week!' Often children's ICT skills are insufficiently developed to enable them to focus on the mathematics. Such issues need to be taken into account if the ICT suite is to be used as an effective teaching context.

Summary

In this chapter we have looked at the importance of excellent pupil–teacher and pupil–pupil interaction for raising the effectiveness of teaching mathematics and examined how a classroom atmosphere that is characterized by a lively mix of discussion, questioning, debate and reasoning can enhance interaction and as a consequence improve the quality of the children's mathematical understanding. Providing the right level of challenge that spurs the children on is also important, as is making connections for the children between the familiar and the novel, the topics within mathematics, such as mathematical concepts and precise mathematical language, and the areas of learning outside mathematics, such as knowledge and understanding of the world or history.

Teachers need to match children's work to their interests and abilities, taking into account any misconceptions that they may have. It is also the teacher's responsibility to provide suitable materials and contexts that are familiar to the pupils so that they remain enthusiastic, motivated and fully engaged with the mathematics. Effective questioning, which is at the heart of a stimulating learning environment, can help to keep children interested and close the gap between what the children already understand and what they need to learn.

Finally, this chapter raises some issues around the use of ICT for mathematics teaching, showing that, while its use will almost certainly have a very positive effect on motivation and enjoyment for the children, the focus must be on its potential to enhance mathematics learning for the children, rather than on the technology itself.

Reflective Questions

- Are you teaching or do you hope to teach using a connectionist model, a transmission model or a discovery model?
- How do you think you can help children to understand the relationships between mathematical topics and between mathematics and other areas of learning?
- Can you think of a misconception that you have had in mathematics? What do you think was the cause?
- How might you use ICT to enhance your teaching of shape and space?

REFERENCES AND FURTHER READING

Askew, M. (1998) *Teaching Primary Mathematics*, London: Hodder and Stoughton.

Askew, M., Brown, M., Rhodes, V., Wiliam, D. and Johnson, D. (1997) 'The contribution of professional development to effectiveness in the teaching of numeracy', *Teacher Development*, 1 (3).

Askew, M. and Wiliam, D. (1995) *Recent Research in Mathematics Education 5–16*, London: HMSO.

Baumfield, V. and Mroz, M. (2002) 'Investigating pupils' questions in the primary classroom', *Educational Research*, 44 (2), Summer, 129–40.

Bruner, J. (1986) *Actual Minds Possible Worlds* London: Harvard University Press.

Denvir, H. and Askew, M. (2001) 'Pupils' participation in the classroom examined in relation to "interactive whole class teaching"', *Proceedings of the British Society for Research into Learning Mathematics*, 21 (1), 25–30.

Koshy, V. (2000) *Effective Teaching in Numeracy for the Mathematics Framework*, London: Hodder and Stoughton.

McGuinness, C. (1999) *From Thinking Skills to Thinking Classrooms: A Review and Evaluation of Approaches for Developing Pupils' Thinking Skills*, DfEE Brief Report No. 115, London: HMSO.

Shuard, H. and Rothery, A. (1984) *Children Reading Mathematics*, London: John Murray.

Thompson, I. (1999) *Issues in Teaching Numeracy in Primary Schools*, Buckingham: Open University Press.

Vygotsky, L. (1978) *Mind in Society*, Cambridge, MA: Harvard University Press.

Resources

INTRODUCTION

Most teachers and pre-school practitioners regard resources as an essential element of teaching and learning mathematics. Although national curricula (where these exist) often specify what is to be taught to children, the resources that are used to accomplish these teaching objectives are often left to the discretion of the individual teacher or practitioner. This approach undoubtedly gives the teacher freedom but also imposes a duty on him or her to make sound professional judgements about the selection and use of resources that will offer the most accessible and rich mathematical learning experience.

In this chapter we will therefore look at:

- The use of mathematical resources
- Purposes of using resources
- Effective use of particular types of resources
- The use of games, stories, role-play and ICT
- Selection and evaluation of resources

Newer teachers and practitioners may lack awareness of the range of available resources, of the subtle mathematical differences that often exist between resources, which may, initially, seem to be similar in nature and function, and of some of the wider implications of using particular resources. We will now consider the purposes of using resources, the types that are available to teachers of mathematics, practical ways in which they may be used and organized in mathematics lessons and the impact that resources have on the wider issues of learning, teaching and assessment. In this chapter, as in the last, the term 'teacher' will again be used to describe anyone who teaches children.

The Use of Mathematical Resources

Among primary school teachers and pre-school practitioners there is a prevailing view that visual representations of mathematical concepts and the manipulation of practical apparatus are helpful in establishing children's understanding of mathematics.

This view is supported, to some extent, by theories of learning and research. Nickson (2000), for example, believes it arises from 'the importance placed on the Piagetian stages in the development of children's thinking'. Jerome Bruner (1966) suggested that there are three modes of representing our experiences: enactive (action-based), iconic (use of physical or mental images) and symbolic (language or symbol-based). It could be argued that in Bruner's notion of enactive and iconic modes the use of resources (objects, pictures or diagrams) in mathematics teaching contributes towards effective development of children's mathematical understanding.

In his well-known 'box task', Martin Hughes (1986) found that very young children, who were unable to perform simple addition and subtraction calculations when they were presented in an abstract manner, were able to perform such calculations when the tasks were presented within the practical context of bricks being placed into or taken out of a box. This was true even when the bricks were hidden inside the box so that the children could not see them. This suggests that the visual image presented by the bricks assisted the children in forming a mental image of the bricks, which represented the numbers involved, and this in turn enabled the children to perform the calculations.

Anghileri (2000: 10) concludes that 'an important stage between the actual manipulation of objects and abstract work is a stage in which objects are imagined'.

Delaney (2001:125) also states that 'there is certainly a consensus that in thoughtful and skilful hands, apparatus of different kinds can help; in fact it is hard to see how some mathematics could be taught without visual or manipulative aids of some kind'.

Although the manipulation of practical apparatus can certainly be helpful in the development of visual images of mathematical concepts, it does have limitations as a support to teaching and learning. It is important to realize that the use of resources is, of itself, insufficient to ensure that learning occurs.

As Gravemeijer (1997) has shown, appreciation of concrete apparatus itself is not the same as making mathematical sense of it.

Similarly, Yackel (2000) formed the view that such resources do not in themselves convey knowledge and that only those who already understand the mathematical concepts being modelled will perceive the mathematics in them, since interpretations of situations are constrained by an individual's prior experiences (Cobb, 1987; Holt, 1982). Delaney (2001: 124) concurs, stating that 'there is no mathematics actually in a resource' but rather 'the mathematics is brought to the resource by those who interact with it or is developed by them as they use it to support or challenge their thinking'. Research by Schoenfeld (1987) demonstrated that even though children may be assisted in their learning of concepts by the use of manipulative apparatus, they are often unable to apply those same concepts in problem-solving situations.

It appears to be generally accepted therefore that children need to progress from working in a largely practical manner to using mental approaches, which can form the basis for more abstract, symbolic work. Thus while classroom resources have a clear role in aiding children's development, it is not enough for the teacher merely to provide and make use of resources and hope that effective learning will occur. Rather, the selection of particular resources, the way in which the resources are used by the teacher and children, the language employed in association with this use, the recognition of the limitations and opportunities offered by resources and the opportunities provided for application of learning in solving problems are all critical aspects of using resources, which an effective teacher must consider.

Purposes of Using Resources

Teachers or children may use resources within mathematics lessons for different purposes. Teachers may use resources to demonstrate, explain and model mathematical ideas, to make connections between aspects of mathematics or as a focus for mathematical discussion. They may also wish to show how mathematics applies to the real world and to provide interest and variety to the children's mathematical experiences. Resources may be used as tools in practical tasks and to support mathematical learning.

Visual representations of mathematical ideas are useful in helping to explain and model mathematical concepts or strategies. The embedding of abstract mathematical ideas within concrete, visible objects can make the underlying mathematics more apparent and much easier to understand and can help children to make the all-important connections between different aspects of mathematics.

It is important to reiterate that it is the teacher's use of the apparatus and of associated mathematical vocabulary that is crucial here and not the apparatus itself.

In research by Bills (2000) the language used by the teacher and the physical representation associated with mental calculation procedures were found to influence the children's own ways of communicating their mental calculation methods.

Use of everyday objects often enables the teacher to show pupils the relevance of mathematics in everyday life and so provides a purpose for mathematical learning. It also helps to extend pupils' understanding of the mathematics involved and enables them to develop 'use and application' skills, so they can apply their mathematical thinking to their own daily lives outside school. As we have seen in previous chapters, mathematics also needs to be set within contexts that are 'meaningful' to children.

 A Chance to Think

For example, pupils aged 10 undertook a survey to discover their peers' preferences for different foods for inclusion in the school meals menu. On the basis of the survey changes to the menu were implemented. This helped the pupils to understand how data handling could be used in making real-life decisions.

A nursery practitioner set up a greengrocer's shop in the role-play area. Patrick and Polly, both 4 years old, were given the task of sorting real vegetables and fruit into different display boxes on the shelves and different coins in the shop till. Later, all the children had the opportunity to be customers at the shop. For many children this was the first opportunity that they had had to use coins for shopping.

It seems to be important that children develop mental imagery if they are fully to appreciate mathematical concepts and processes (see Chapter 2). Anghileri (2000) suggests that 'classroom materials provide powerful images', which can assist mathematical development. Children's mental representations may also be heavily influenced by the verbal, pictorial, written and concrete representations used by their teachers (Bills, 1999). Appropriateness of resources selected could, in this context, be judged by the extent to which the mental images that children may form as a result are likely to be helpful or unhelpful in structuring their thinking and the degree of flexibility of thought that these mental images will permit. For example, a number track may be useful for children attempting early addition and subtraction work because it models the counting numbers and so may be used to help them in their calculations. (See the section below on selection and evaluation of resources for an example of a number track.)

Using resources can also provide opportunities to stimulate discussion of mathematical ideas with or among the whole class or a group of children engaged on a collaborative task.

Children can work together very productively if they are provided with stimulating and interesting resources. Peter and Gary, for example, were using pieces of fabric as part of a science investigation on the strengths of materials. They became interested in the pattern and symmetry of the designs on the pieces of fabric and spent some time discussing these. Later they also used their mathematical knowledge to construct a graph showing what they had found from their investigation of strength of materials. Another group in the class were given the task of interpreting their data so that they could replicate Peter and Gary's work and make further tests of their own. Thus the children were involved in practical, collaborative problem-solving activity, recording and interpreting data, making mathematical predictions and conjectures and discussing trends in the data.

In general, using resources to provide diversity usually increases motivation, which may result in enhanced learning. More specifically, there are some aspects of mathematics, such as shape concepts, in which variety in the resources provided is essential for effective learning. For example, Orton and Frobisher (1996) suggest that 'A young pupil, having triangles and other polygons of various shapes, sizes and colours, … is more likely to understand the properties of triangles than the pupil who has been given only red triangular shapes.' This is because children often make generalizations when they believe they have spotted common patterns or key features of a mathematical concept. If the teacher has provided an insufficient variety of examples, these generalizations may be incorrect. Askew and Wiliam (1995) develop this idea further by noting that in order to help children develop understanding of a mathematical concept they must be given both examples and non-examples of the concept, so that they realize which features of the examples provided are relevant and which are irrelevant to the concept being studied. This has clear implications for the selection of resources.

Children may use resources, when learning mathematics, as tools in practical tasks. Such tools could range from measuring devices to ICT tools; they may be an intrinsic requirement for completion of specific mathematical tasks, such as a metre rule for measuring the length of the room; or they may simply be the most appropriate tool for the task in hand, for example counters or unifix bricks for working out simple multiplication. Of course, children need to be shown how to use such resources reliably and efficiently. They also need to learn how to select the most suitable resources, for example, whether they should use a metre rule or a 10 metre tape to measure the playground, and to be given opportunities to justify their selections.

Resources can be used to support the modelling of mathematical ideas (see Chapter 3) and children can often use the same (or smaller versions of) apparatus as the teacher had used earlier in a lesson.

 A Chance to Think

Winston and Lara had been watching their teacher use a large number track and a floor robot to demonstrate addition. The floor robot was programmed first by the teacher and later by some children to add small numbers. The teacher then gave Winston and Lara a small number track and a play person so that they could make up their own additions and work out the answers using a smaller version of the number track.

Children may also find resources useful when articulating their mathematical ideas and understanding to the teacher or to other children. This may occur in discussions where they are asked to justify their answers to the teacher or where they have to convince other children about their approach or solution in a collaborative task.

In a collaborative problem-solving task, for example, six children were asked to shake hands with each other just once and count the number of handshakes exchanged. Karim recognized that the number of handshakes would be equal to $1 + 2 + 3 + 4 + 5 + 6$ and that these numbers could be added quickly by adding together pairs of numbers that make 7. He created some 'towers' of interlocking cubes (as shown opposite) and then rearranged them to support his explanation to his peers that the total number of handshakes would be $(6 + 1) + (5 + 2) + (4 + 3) = 3 \times 7 = 21$.

The handshake problem

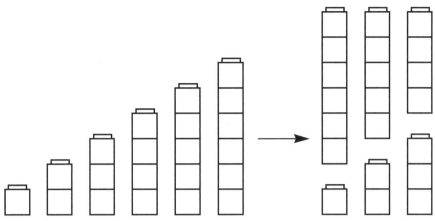

Effective Use of Particular Types of Resources

There are broadly two types of mathematical apparatus that can be used to support children's learning, namely structured and unstructured.

Structured mathematical apparatus is designed specifically as an embodiment of a particular mathematical conceptual structure and therefore manipulations of the materials by child or teacher directly reflect the equivalent mathematical manipulations within that structure. They are designed to eliminate distracting features.

Dienes's base ten materials have traditionally been used as an embodiment of our base ten place-value system and are therefore an example of structured apparatus that can be used to model various aspects of number.

For example, the process of decomposition in subtraction algorithms for calculating, say, 754–582, can be modelled as shown on page 88 using base ten apparatus:

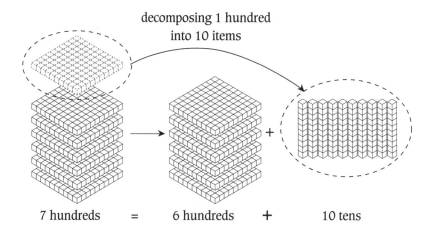

decomposing 1 hundred
into 10 items

7 hundreds   =   6 hundreds   +   10 tens

A particular piece of structured apparatus can therefore be used to model the associated mathematical conceptual structure or strategy. It is commonly accepted that such apparatus may be particularly beneficial in helping children to develop their own understanding of the associated mathematics because of the one-to-one correspondence between the apparatus and the aspect of mathematics being studied. This helps children in the formulation of mental images, which, as we have alredy seen, can then aid them in tackling the mathematics at a later stage without the support of the physical apparatus.

This sounds very simple but there are, nevertheless, issues to consider when using this type of equipment and children may not always understand the link between the apparatus and the particular mathematical concept it is designed to demonstrate.

Frobisher *et al.* (1999: 22) suggest that 'having this embedded structure does not guarantee that children will perceive its existence, nor will they necessarily abstract it in such a way that it is assimilated into their schema' and therefore the teacher must 'articulate the relationship between the embedded structure and its representation'. Threfall (1996) indicates that teachers may assume that in using such apparatus to support children's understanding, that that they are teaching mathematics when, in fact, they may only be teaching children to manipulate or use the apparatus itself.

Similarly, it is possible for children to become overdependent on the apparatus as a support for their thinking and so it is important that they 'develop mental imagery associated with these materials' in order that they may 'work with "imagined" situations' (Anghileri, 2000). Furthermore, there is the danger that because these materials have no place in everyday life children may 'not relate their classroom interactions with the associated use of structured materials to their existing out-of-school problem-solving'

(Aubrey, 1997: 26) thus limiting the scope of their learning. Thus when using structured apparatus, it is important to make a point of associating what children are learning to the mathematical contexts they experience outside the school context.

Sometimes, it is more helpful to use unstructured apparatus to support mathematics teaching and learning. Unstructured apparatus does not have an underlying structure that mirrors a corresponding mathematical conceptual structure. This can be useful when we want to avoid imposing structure on a child's understanding at too early a stage and thus allow children the freedom to explore.

 A Chance to Think

Emily and Darvinda were 3 and their teacher wanted to find out what they knew about sorting. At first she gave them some unstructured sets of random objects to sort, such as a pencil, a jug and a toy. Later in the school term they progressed to sorting structured sets of objects, for example, toy farm animals and coloured regular shapes.

We can find many examples of successful use of unstructured apparatus when trying to relate mathematics teaching or learning to everyday life. David, a teacher, showed the children in his class a piece of wrapping paper as a stimulus for discussing how mathematical ideas about pattern such as symmetry, reflection, rotation and translation are used in everyday life. Davina and Victor, aged 8, took apart a cube-shaped tissue box to see how it was constructed and to look at the net (the box opened completely and laid flat). This led them to wonder whether they could make this type of box any other way. They thought that there were several different ways that the box could be made. Their teacher then asked them how many possible ways there were and they went on to investigate by drawing all the possible nets for a cube on squared paper.

Because they are familiar to children, everyday resources such as wrapping paper or toy cars are less abstract than resources that are specifically manufactured for the mathematics classroom and which children do not encounter in real-life contexts. Objects drawn from real life should not be dismissed in favour of more structured materials as everyday objects can be very valuable in enabling children to recognize that mathematics is purposeful and useful in everyday life, to understand that mathematics can be used as a tool to model and interpret different aspects of life and to apply the mathematics they are learning. They also make them realize, for example, that everything has a shape, not just the cubes and spheres that are kept in the box in the classroom marked 'shapes'.

Amy and Warwick were asked to build with real junk boxes in order to explore aspects of three-dimensional shape (such as rolling, stacking, size and stability). These were more effective than commercially produced shapes because they had more meaning to the children. The teacher helped the children to make connections to familiar everyday examples, such as shelf-stacking in the supermarket or the shapes used in local buildings.

The use of unstructured resources in well-planned role play provides key opportunities for young children to learn with enjoyment. Role play enables children to try out ideas without the fear of failure and to experience mathematics in pseudo-real contexts that mirror those from the real world, which they know.

Griffiths (1994: 146) indicates that play-based activity gives a purpose for learning, provides a concrete context for mathematics and enables children to practise in a pressure-free environment. Pound (1999: 69) suggests that in such play, whether alone or with friends, children are 'practising, rehearsing and representing things that they have seen, heard and experienced' and that this lays the foundations for mathematical thinking.

The teacher's role is crucial in offering challenging and rich environments for children to explore through role play. In particular, the number and variety of resources supplied for the children within the role-play area will determine to a large extent the nature and the range of learning opportunities that are available for children to develop their understanding of mathematical concepts and associated vocabulary and for the teacher to consolidate, extend and assess children's understanding through play-partnering, questioning and observing.

A Chance to Think

A teacher created a role play based on the three bears' cottage from 'Goldilocks and the Three Bears' in order to enable the children to learn about aspects of length and mass. It included the following resources:

- miniature beds with matching blankets in three sizes
- chairs in three sizes
- eating utensils (bowls, knives, forks, spoons, cups, etc.) in three sizes placed on a table

The children (and teacher) were thus able to explore direct comparison and ordering of the three bears' property for both length and mass and, in addition, the associated vocabulary (e.g. longest, shortest, highest, heaviest, lightest, longer, shorter, heavier, lighter).

Among the questions about length the teacher asked were 'Who has the longest bed/ the smallest chair?', 'Can you make a bed for baby bear?', 'Which is the longest spoon?', 'Can you put the spoons beside the right bowls on the table?', 'Which is the shortest way to the three bears' cottage?' and 'How do you know that this blanket is for this bed?'

In relation to mass the children explored questions such as 'Who has the lightest chair?', 'Will this bowl be heavier than baby bear's?' and 'How can I find out?'

Children's story books also offer a wide range of mathematical learning opportunities for the teacher who is aware of the possibilities. Many story books contain scenarios, illustrations and vocabulary relating to mathematical ideas such as aspects of quantity, time, size, position, movement, probability, sequencing, pattern or shapes. Pound (1999: 13) suggests that use of such stories offers opportunities for children to 'reiterate vital vocabulary'. In addition, many stories include elements of repetition, which children can be invited to anticipate or predict. For very young children, stories can also provide a meaningful context in which further mathematical opportunities, such as role-play activities or small-world play, can be offered by the teacher. In this way 'the language of story is supported by physical action' (Pound, 1999: 62). Mathematical problem-solving or investigation activities can also be developed from stories.

 A Chance to Think

Janice, the teacher, reads a story about a giant. The children are asked to imagine the giant and to consider how big the giant might be. Janice then provides a stimulus for the children in the form of an imprint of a giant's hand. The children are asked to estimate the height of the giant. They proceed to compare the giant's handprint with their own handprints and then use ratios to calculate an estimate for the giant's height.

The UK government has provided a helpful list of children's story books that can be used for developing children's understanding of mathematics, available from http://www. standards.dfes.gov.uk/ numeracy/NNSresources/stories/.

Board games and other commercially or teacher-produced games, if used judiciously, can be an effective means of providing children with opportunities for exploring mathematical relationships and strategies (Anghileri, 2000: 13) and providing opportunities for reinforcement and practice of aspects of mathematics (Parr, 1994: 29).

For many children games also offer an informal, non-threatening context, which may help to sustain their motivation and confidence and thus their engagement with mathematics. They quite often provide a link with the home where board or other games might be played as a leisure activity. Games may also provide children with a purpose for using the mathematics they are learning, since achieving success within the context of the game is likely to be important, and therefore meaningful or 'real' to them (Ainley, 1988: 243).

From a teacher's perspective, games require children to engage in discussion about the mathematics inherent in the game and thus they 'present teachers with opportunities for listening to children' (Anghileri, 2000: 13) with a view to assessing their mathematical thinking. This concurs with Ainley's (1988: 248) view that 'when children are playing games their thinking is much more transparent'.

Some mathematical games provide opportunities for developing children's knowledge and use of key mathematical skills such as predicting, conjecturing, generalizing, justifying and investigating. For example, predicting the consequences of a particular decision or move, conjecturing about and evaluating particular strategies for winning, recognizing patterns, possibilities and impossibilities, justifying personal strategies and challenging the mathematics of another player are all useful learning experiences that games may offer. In addition, many games lend themselves to opportunities for children to engage in open-ended investigation by tackling questions relating to changes in the parameters of games. Investigating what would happen if the rules were changed in particular ways or evaluating the effects of changing the number of players, the shape of a game board or the target for winning and deciding if the game would still be fair are examples of this. Naturally, if children are to exploit these opportunities, they need to be allowed to play a particular game over and over again.

The most effective games are those in which mathematics is embedded within the structure of the game and 'where winning the game is directly related to understanding this mathematics' (Ainley, 1988: 241).

A Chance to Think

Compare the following games:

Game 1: Jaz and Ruth were playing a game that involves moving a counter around a track consisting of numbered squares. On landing on certain squares, the children were required to pick up a card from a pack of cards, each of which had a two-digit addition or subtraction calculation written upon it. When the calculation was answered correctly the child was allowed to move her counter a further five squares towards the final square. Ruth reached the final square first and so was the winner.

Game 2: Suzanne and Gavin were playing a game in which each of them had five cards, each inscribed with a number between ten and 30. They were required to try to link all five of the numbers on their cards within a series of addition and subtraction calculations to produce a number as close as possible to 20 (a target the teacher had selected). The children were required to check each other's attempts to reach the target number.

At face value the two games might appear to be equally valid, focusing on number operations involving two-digit numbers. However, the first game is much more limited, in that the structure of the game is principally based on counting squares around a track and therefore winning the game is not intrinsically about using addition or subtraction calculation strategies. In comparison, in Game 2 the use of addition and subtraction strategies is a key part of winning the game. Furthermore, in contrast to Game 1, Game 2 allows for much more creativity and encourages mental flexibility, as the five numbers held by each child can be combined in a variety of ways using a variety of mental addition and subtraction strategies.

It is important to realize that involvement in playing mathematical games will not, of itself, teach children mathematics. As with any resource, 'the teacher's role in stimulating mathematical learning during the playing of a game, and monitoring the learning which is going on, is vital' (Ainley, 1988: 243).

In many schools commercially published mathematics schemes are a common resource. They usually consist of a series of children's textbooks or work cards accompanied by a teacher's manual. Many such schemes now also include additional resources such as photocopy masters, computer software or whole-class teaching resources.

This type of resource can be useful if used in a selective way but one of the potential dangers of using such schemes is that the teacher may allow the materials to determine their teaching of mathematics. Over-reliance on a particular published scheme may also lead to pupils spending prolonged periods of time working at a slow pace on repetitive, undemanding tasks that do little to advance their understanding or proficiency (OfSTED, 1993: 16). It is better, therefore, to use the published scheme materials only when a particular part of the scheme is the best resource available for supporting children in achieving the learning objectives for a lesson, rather than expect children to work through the materials in a sequential, page-by-page manner.

When deciding whether or not to use materials from a published scheme there are a number of issues to consider. It is important to evaluate the readability of the pupil materials (complexity of language used, layout on a page), the visual presentation of the mathematics involved (pictures, words, symbols), the methods of recording expected and the degree of provision of opportunities for practical work, consolidation exercises, investigative or problem-solving activities and discussion.

A common use of such materials is to provide independent activities for some children in the classroom so as to enable the teacher to work in a focused way with other children. However, it is possible to use such schemes more creatively.

For example, within a scheme workbook that Jane had in her cupboard, she found some pages that required the children to write number story patterns. She used one of the pages to set a group of children a challenge. She gave each of the children a copy of the number story of ten and ten bricks. She asked the children to complete the number story and then to look at the patterns to see what they noticed. The children noticed that there were patterns of descending and ascending numbers and as one row of numbers went up the other went down. They then set about trying to explain why this might be.

The Use of ICT

A wide variety of information and communications technologies can be used in the teaching and learning of mathematics, e.g. computers, calculators, programmable robots, television, radio, video, the Internet, data-logging equipment, data projectors, overhead projectors and digital cameras. Teachers need to be able to use ICT for two different kinds of purposes, namely, as a tool (like any other resource) for enhancing children's learning of the subject and as a tool for professional purposes other than teaching (such as planning and record-keeping). This section considers only the former.

While not all mathematics lessons will involve the use of ICT, ICT should be used where it is appropriate, i.e. as an effective means of achieving mathematical teaching and learning objectives (but not, as we have said earlier, as a means of practising ICT skills). Pupils' ages, attainments and prior experiences (including those gained outside school) are key issues to consider in relation to the suitability of ICT resources. You should also bear in mind aspects of ICT resources that could affect pupils' ability to use or respond to it (for example, the level of sophistication of language used, the degree of responsiveness and of interactivity offered, the clarity of presentation, etc.). When planning, there will also be issues such as the organization of the use of the ICT resource, health and safety, the monitoring and assessment of children's progress and opportunities for teacher intervention to consider. Equally, you should think about providing opportunities for mathematics activities that do not use ICT but are related to those undertaken using ICT devices.

The following are appropriate uses of ICT within a mathematics lesson:

- exploring an aspect of mathematics which is enhanced, more apparent or made possible by the dynamic interactive nature of ICT
- practising and consolidating mathematical knowledge and skills
- manipulating data and images in mathematical ways, both rapidly and efficiently
- exploring patterns and trends
- developing logical thinking (e.g. in problem-solving or controlling a programmable floor robot such as floor turtle)
- learning from immediate feedback and using it as a basis for improved strategies (sometimes known as trial and improvement)
- developing skills in presenting and communicating mathematical information
- developing mental skills, e.g. mentally calculating numbers or visualizing the outcome produced by rotating a shape
- enabling children with special educational needs to access some aspects of mathematics that would otherwise be inaccessible or supporting children who have mathematics-specific needs

In situations where ICT is to be used by pupils, the type of organization employed will depend on the type and amount of ICT equipment available as well as the nature of the activity. If several pupils are to use one piece of equipment, the teacher must ensure that all the pupils are actively engaged and learning and that appropriate interventions are made.

Sometimes the teacher may use ICT equipment as a teaching resource either to demonstrate or model an aspect of mathematics, or as a focus for mathematical discussion, interpretation, prediction or generalization. Both of these contexts could involve the teacher working with a group of children as an activity within the mathematics lesson or, alternatively, the teacher working with the whole class, for example using a computer with a large monitor or data projector or using a television programme as a basis for mathematical discussion. Discussions within the lesson could focus on the mathematics offered by the use of ICT equipment.

For example, a teacher presents a graph about the effect of watering on plant growth produced on a computer during a previous science lesson. This provides a context for assessing or developing pupils' ability to interpret the data gathered. The teacher asks questions ranging in difficulty from easier questions such as 'Which plant grew the most?' to harder questions such as 'What do you think would happen if we watered the plant twice as much?' or 'How might the graph be different if the plants had been placed in direct sunlight?'

It is quite possible for pupils to produce very presentable and accurate work using ICT resources with only limited understanding of the relevant mathematics. Thus, teachers do need to be aware of what the ICT resource may do for the child (for example, automatic scaling of graphs) without the child's having to understand. Failure to recognize these 'features' of ICT resources could mean that the teacher's assessment of a child's attainment and progress may be flawed. Consequently, when planning assessments of mathematical attainment based on use of ICT resources one needs to plan assessments that will not be compromised by those aspects that may mask a child's true attainment. Similarly, when children are working collaboratively with an ICT resource, you need to be able to distinguish between the contributions (and corresponding mathematical understanding) of the pupils involved.

As with all resources, the teacher must give due consideration and thought to the relevance of the resource to the planned teaching and learning.

Selection and Evaluation of Resources

The resources used for any particular mathematics teaching and learning should be related to the nature of the task being undertaken, the type of learning or teaching that is expected and the way in which the children are to be organized. Most mathematics lessons will employ a variety of teaching and learning strategies and the class is likely to be organized according to whether the teacher wishes to encourage whole-class interactive teaching, collaborative group work or individual work. This will to some extent determine the suitability of resources.

A wide variety of resources exist for the purpose of teaching and learning mathematics, some specifically designed with mathematical teaching and learning in mind and others not. In addition, the same resource may be used differently in different lessons and/or serve a different purpose in different phases of a particular lesson.

When selecting apparatus to use in a lesson you should consider the extent to which the apparatus matches or differs from the mathematics the teacher intends to model. To illustrate this, we will consider two common classroom resources, namely, number tracks and number lines.

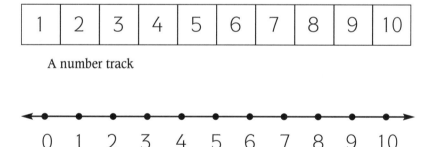

A number track

A number line

At first glance the number track looks very similar in appearance to the number line. However, there are subtle differences, which have implications for their use by teachers in the classroom.

The squares on a number track are countable and the number within any square corresponds to the number of squares counted so far (starting from one). It would be tempting in some contexts to include zero on a number track and unfortunately many commercially produced number tracks do include zero. However, the inclusion of zero would undermine the square–number correspondence when counting for, as soon as you count the square in which the zero resides you have counted one square, yet your counting finger is pointing at the zero. Thus, zero should not be included on a number track, nor, for similar reasons, should integers less than zero (such as -1, -2, -3, etc.). Furthermore, the numbers on a number track (and the countable squares) are discrete; it is impossible to locate intermediate values such as $3\frac{1}{4}$ or 5·7. We may conclude, therefore, that whereas the number track is ideal for supporting the development of simple counting and of simple addition and subtraction strategies based on counting (such as counting on or counting back), it is too simplistic a representation of the number system to be used as a model when teaching children about negative numbers, fractions or decimals.

By comparison, the image offered by a number line is one of equal spacings or lengths between successive integers. It is the distance along the number line that determines the numerical value of a particular point on the line and thus when using a number line we are concerned with measuring (rather than counting). Because of this, the number-line representation of the number system permits the inclusion of zero and so we can extend the number line to include negative integers.

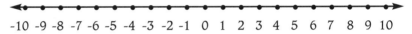

-10 -9 -8 -7 -6 -5 -4 -3 -2 -1 0 1 2 3 4 5 6 7 8 9 10

In addition, it is continuous (i.e. between any two values there is always an intermediate value) and so all intermediate values can be represented, making the number line a useful model to use when teaching about fractions and decimals.

Finally, it is possible to use just a part of the number line, say the numbers between 52 and 87 or between -10 and 10, as above. Doing this with a number track would destroy the number–square correspondence that is an intrinsic part of its representation of the counting numbers. The number track is ideal for supporting young children's counting-based strategies, but the number line is obviously more versatile because it models the number system more closely than the number track.

A more recent model pioneered in the Netherlands for use in the teaching of number is that of an 'empty number line', which has no intervals and no numbers marked on it.

Empty number-line strategies for calculating 82 – 26

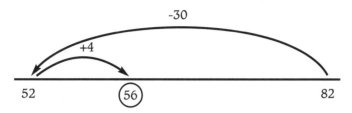

Using a compensation strategy

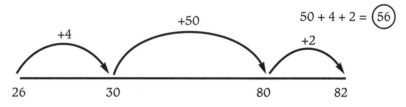

Using counting on (complementary addition)

Research by Streefland (1991) has shown that the empty number line enables children to be flexible in the size of jumps, large jumps being indicated as easily as small jumps (see Chapter 2). Anghileri (1997: 50) claims that 'since the children may decide the starting and stopping points and need not work to scale, they are able to develop mental imagery that goes beyond the unit intervals normally found on number lines'. This suggests that the empty number-line model has greater flexibility than the traditional number line and children can exploit this in supporting their mental calculation strategies. However, the teacher must also bear in mind that in using the empty number-line model children must forgo the greater structure of the scale (which indicates the relative sizes of numbers and the differences between them) of the traditional number line. Thus, the empty number line has distinct advantages over the traditional number line for a child who has sufficient awareness of the relationships between numbers but would be a very unsuitable resource for a child who did not have such facility with number.

More generally, when selecting resources to support teaching or learning it is important for the teacher to consider the degree to which a particular resource may model, fail to model or even contradict aspects of the mathematical concept or strategy that the teacher is trying to teach.

For example, a teacher presenting a lesson on place value may be justified in using place-value cards as a resource to model the partitioning of two-digit numbers into tens and ones but place-value cards would not be a good way to provide a sense of the size of particular numbers because the numbers on the cards are purely symbolic in nature.

Poor selection of resources by the teacher may contribute to or give rise to the development of misconceptions by children, which sometimes may not become apparent until later. For example, children always presented with triangles that have a horizontal base will have difficulty recognizing triangles in other orientations.

 ### A Chance to Think

James was teaching a lesson about tessellation and provided children with a box of flat shapes. The only pentagons in the box were regular pentagons. The textbook used in the lesson had images of regular pentagons in one orientation only.

The children were asked to decide which polygons would tessellate and which would not. The children tried to tessellate with the regular pentagons in the box and discovered that they would not tessellate. On the basis of this experience, the children concluded that there are no pentagons that tessellate.

Had there been some irregular pentagons included in the box of shapes, the children might have reached the correct conclusion that regular pentagons will not tessellate but that some irregular pentagons, though not all, will tessellate. The obvious lesson is that the teacher should provide a wider range of pentagons to avoid overgeneralization on the basis of a limited range of pentagons

When teaching concepts, teachers should select resources so as to provide examples of the concept that 'rule in' as much as possible and non-examples that 'rule out' as much as possible, in order to minimize the extent to which children may associate irrelevant features with the concept (Askew and Wiliam, 1995: 14–15). For example, if teaching children about rectangles it would be important to offer examples such as shapes A (a rectangle that is also a square) and B (a rectangle in non-vertical or horizontal orientation), as well as to show examples of near-rectangles such as shapes C (has two pairs of opposite parallel sides but not four right angles) and D (has four straight sides but not all are parallel and there are only three right angles).

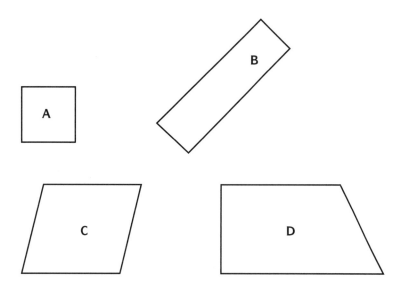

Children sometimes use a resource in way that is not intended by the teacher. Furthermore, they may achieve the desired answers by using the resource differently but fail to learn the mathematics that the teacher expected they would learn. This absence of expected learning may go undetected by the teacher. For example, Dan and Marcus were provided with some blocks to aid them in solving the problem, 'how many biscuits in four packages of biscuits if there are three biscuits in each package?' The teacher expected the children to set out the blocks as four groups of three blocks and hoped that this would support their developing understanding of multiplication. The children achieved the correct answer but did so simply by counting the bricks. They failed to appreciate the multiplicative aspects of the task. If the teacher were to assess the children's learning purely by marking their written answers, then he or she might reach a false conclusion about the extent of the children's understanding of multiplication. It is clear, therefore, that the teacher must monitor the use of any resource provided for children. In addition, provision of resources may, in some circumstances, encourage children to revert back to lower-level strategies within mathematical situations.

Summary

Although it is generally accepted that children's learning of mathematics progresses from dealing with the concrete (physical objects or situations) to handling the abstract (using symbols, formal language, generalizations, etc.), it is less certain how to accelerate such development. Recent research shows that teachers need to devise ways of linking the 'situated informal knowledge of children' (Gravemeijer, 1997) with the more formal mathematical concepts that they wish children to learn.

Resources are believed to play an important part in supporting children's developing understanding of mathematics. However, children do not necessarily perceive the mathematical structures within the resources that teachers expect them to perceive. The role of the teacher is, therefore, crucial in articulating and attributing meaning to the use of resources when modelling and discussing mathematical concepts and strategies. Furthermore, teachers need to present a wide variety of examples and non-examples of concepts to expose existing misconceptions and to prevent the formation of new ones. It is also vital that teachers consider, when planning a lesson, the extent to which a particular resource models, fails to model or conflicts with the concept they are attempting to teach.

Appropriate resources are important, but this is not an end to the matter. The way that the class is organized and managed will also have considerable impact on the children's mathematical learning.

Reflective Questions

- What resources could you use in the classroom to support the teaching of multiplication and how would these resources reflect the concepts that you want the children to acquire?
- Can you identify the differences between a number track and a number line?
- What mathematical games do you have in your class and what mathematical processes might the children learn or practise by their use?
- How can you use the classroom and/or the outside play space to encourage mathematical play?

REFERENCES AND FURTHER READING

Ainley, J. (1988) 'Playing games and real mathematics', in Pimm, D. (ed.) *Mathematics, Teachers and Children,* London: Hodder and Stoughton/Open University Press.

Anghileri, J. (2000) *Teaching Number Sense*, London: Continuum.

Anghileri, J. (1997) 'Uses of counting in multiplication and division', in Thompson, I. (ed.) *Teaching and Learning Early Number*, Buckingham: Open University Press.

Askew, M. and Wiliam, D. (1995) *Recent Research in Mathematics Education*, London: HMSO.

Aubrey, C. (1997) 'Children's early learning of number in school and out', in Thompson, I. (ed.) *Teaching and Learning Early Number*, Buckingham: Open University Press.

Bills, C.J. (1999) 'What was in your head when you were thinking of that?', *Mathematics Teaching*, 168, pp. 39–41.

Bills, C.J. (2000) 'Metaphors and other Linguistic Pointers to Children's Mental Representations', in Morgan, C. and Jones, K. (eds) *Research into Mathematics Education Volume 3: Papers of the British Society for Research into Learning Mathematics*, London: British Society for Research into Learning Mathematics.

Bruner, J. (1966) 'On cognitive growth', in Bruner, J., Oliver, R. and Greenfield, P. (eds) *Studies in Cognitive Growth*, New York: John Wiley.

Cobb, P. (1987) 'Information-processing psychology and mathematics education – a constructivist perspective', *The Journal of Mathematical Behaviour*, 6, 3–40.

Delaney, K. (2001) 'Teaching Mathematics Resourcefully', in Gates, P. (ed.) *Issues in Mathematics Teaching*, London: Routledge Falmer.

Frobisher, L. *et al.* (1999) *Learning to Teach Number*, Cheltenham: Stanley Thorne.

Griffiths, R. (1994) 'Mathematics and Play', in Moyles, J. (ed.) *The Excellence of Play*, Buckingham: Open University Press.

Gravemeijer, K. (1997) 'Mediating between the concrete and abstract', in Nunes, T. and Bryant, P. (eds) *Learning and Teaching Mathematics: An International Perspective*, Hove, Sussex: Psychology Press.

Holt, J. (1982) *How Children Fail*, revised edition, New York: Dell Publishing Co.

Hughes, M. (1986) *Children and Number*, Oxford: Blackwell.

Nickson, M. (2000) *Teaching and Learning Mathematics*, London: Cassell.

Ofsted (1993) *The Teaching and Learning of Early Number in Primary Schools*, London: HMSO.

Orton, A. and Frobisher, L. (1996) *Insights into Teaching Mathematics*, London: Continuum.

Parr, A. (1994) 'Games for playing', *Mathematics in School*, 23 (3), 29–30.

Pound, L. (1999) *Supporting Mathematical Development in the Early Years*, Buckingham: Open University Press.

Schoenfeld, A. (1987) 'What's all the fuss about metacognition?', in Schoenfeld, A. (ed.) *Cognitive Science and Mathematics Education*, Hillsdale, NJ: Lawrence Erlbaum Associates.

Streefland, L. (1991) *Realistic Mathematics Education in Primary School*, The Hague: CIP–Gegevens Koninklijke Bibliotheek.

Threfall, J. (1996) 'The role of practical apparatus in the teaching and learning of arithmetic', *Educational Review*, 48 (1), 3–12.

Yackel, E. (2000) 'Perspectives on arithmetic from classroom-based research in the USA', in Anghileri, J. (ed.) *Principles and Practices in Arithmetic Teaching*, Buckingham: Open University Press.

Organizing and Managing Mathematics

INTRODUCTION

The effective teaching and learning of mathematics in the pre-school and in primary classrooms are reliant on several factors, and cannot be attributed solely to the planning, content and delivery of individual lessons.

If children are to reach their full potential then the teacher or practitioner needs to ensure that the needs of the children are met. Catering successfully for the needs of each and every individual child is not easy but can be more effective if a variety of teaching strategies, organizational methods and aspects of classroom management, is considered alongside the preparation of mathematical content and delivery.

This chapter explores the following topics:

- Organizing the children and effective pupil groupings
- Differentiation
- Enhancing pupil participation
- Ensuring and maintaining effective classroom management
- Managing discussion in classroom mathematics
- Managing misconceptions in mathematics

- Managing mathematical play
- Managing resources and ICT in the mathematics classroom
- Managing other adults
- Marking, assessment and target setting

Organizing the Children and Effective Pupil Groupings

How you plan for a mathematics lesson will depend to some extent on the age of the children. In the case of children aged between 3 and 5 (in England the Foundation Stage) you would usually plan around intended mathematics learning outcomes but give children the space to explore other related areas if they so wish.

When planning a mathematics lesson in a more formal situation for older children (Key Stages 1 and 2 of the English system), you would decide what you want to teach and how the children will best learn (Pollard, 2002). The first priority is likely to be the establishment of mathematical learning objectives for the session. Once the intended outcomes have been determined, you need to decide how to organize or group the children. This will depend upon the activity that you want the children to engage in and on the previous experience of the children. It is easy to see that different pupil groupings will be effective at different times and for different activities.

Children can be organized in a variety of ways such as a whole-class group, alongside other children in a small group, cooperatively as a small group, with a partner or as individuals. Small groups can be arranged to comprise children with similar abilities or children with mixed abilities. The responsibility for choosing the most beneficial method of organization rests with the teachers, so teachers must be flexible and consider grouping carefully, to ensure that effective teaching and learning occur.

 A Chance to Think

The teacher asked the class to work together in pairs on an activity looking at near doubles. Emma and Michelle were given a mini whiteboard and felt-tip pen each and were asked to complete the same doubles questions. Michelle had to double the numbers as they were, and Emma had to use the near-double strategy and compensate. For example, both girls would be given the sum 9 + 9. Michelle would calculate mentally 9 + 9, but Emma would calculate 10 + 10 and compensate by taking away 2. The first person to complete the sums would stop the other. Michelle and Emma would then check their answers with a calculator and talk about the most efficient and effective method.

There are four main ways in which children might be grouped for mathematical work:

- Whole-class group
- Small group
- Pairs
- Individuals

In England, the introduction of the National Numeracy strategy has encouraged teachers to introduce the three-part lesson, which begins and ends with whole-class teaching and discussion. Whole-class grouping is beneficial when direct, interactive teaching is taking place such as during the exposition of mathematical ideas or processes by the teacher and also during parts of the lesson when questioning is required or children are sharing their mathematical understanding with the whole class. Some teachers engage their children in mathematical warm-up sessions before the main teaching, and whole-class teaching would be appropriate for this. Foundation Stage children can also take part in whole-class sessions but these will usually be shorter in duration.

 A Chance to Think

Teresa, the class teacher, gave each of the children a card that was divided into eight squares and in each square there was a number between zero and 20. Teresa had prepared a number of questions ranging from fairly easy additions to multiplication and division. Unbeknown to the children, Teresa had graded the cards in relation to the questions, so that some cards had the answers to the easier questions and some to the more difficult. In this way all the children were able to take part at their own level of understanding. Each time a question was asked, the children with the answer covered it with a counter. The children had to call out when all their numbers were covered. The children were all motivated by this task, which was non-threatening and matched to their individual learning needs. The cards were used over and over again by the children in Teresa's class, as all that she had to do was to produce an alternative set of questions each time.

Whole-class grouping is also relevant during parts of the lesson where previous knowledge is being recounted and mathematical aspects are being reviewed and consolidated. Children's understanding can be enhanced by providing a consolidation period towards the end of the lesson, in which the teacher will have the opportunity to recap on the learning that has taken place and set the scene for future learning. There may be also be times during mathematics lessons when bringing together the children as a whole group is desirable. This may be to iron out misconceptions as they occur and to re-establish the focus of the lesson or to celebrate a new idea or the modelling of a process.

 A Chance to Think

The teacher, Mrs Chandler, set the children off on their task. They were working in pairs to identify relevant key words and phrases within set word problems. The children were asked to read the word problems together and highlight the important words or facts that would help them complete the calculations. However, the children were asked not to complete the actual calculations. While monitoring the children at work, Mrs Chandler noticed that several pairs were highlighting redundant information and that it would be best to deal with the issue as a whole class rather than with each pair. She therefore stopped the whole class and asked them to look towards her while she modelled the process again. However, she was careful to draw upon those pairs that were successfully completing the task and therefore approached the situation positively. This ensured a discreet approach towards ironing out misconceptions and misunderstandings. After modelling the process, Mrs Chandler asked the children to recheck their completed work before continuing with the task.

Small-group, paired or individual work is appropriate either for short points for discussion in whole-class work or once a main whole-class teaching session has been carried out and children know exactly what they have been asked to do and how to achieve the desired outcome.

Encouraging small groups of three or four children to work together ensures that all children within the group have the opportunity to work collaboratively to develop the social and communication skills that are essential in any primary classroom, as well as developing mathematical vocabulary and a more secure negotiated understanding. The essential component in small-group work is collaboration between the children. This type of grouping should not be confused with children working individually alongside each other on a similar task. Younger children will often choose their own informal groups but as they enter school proper the teacher will usually decide who works with whom. There are two main ways of organizing small-group work. The first of these is children working in mixed-ability groups and the second is children working with peers who are deemed to be of similar mathematical ability.

Mixed-ability grouping is not often seen in primary classrooms in England but it does have a number of advantages for the children. It benefits those needing support, as well as those needing to consolidate their understanding or undertake a challenge. Children in mixed-ability groups can all contribute at their own level of understanding. There are opportunities for the child with more developed understanding to break down conceptual understanding into manageable pieces in order to explain their strategies, thus strengthening or reinforcing their thinking. Children who have less understanding can be scaffolded by their more knowledgeable peers; thus both parties benefit from the teaching and learning experience. Furthermore, mixed-ability group work can promote higher self-esteem in those children who find mathematics difficult, where working with more knowledgeable peers can assist in building confidence and reduce anxiety.

Pollard (2002) identifies four different types of groups.

- Task groups – where a group of children work together on a task allocated to them by the teacher
- Teaching groups – where the teacher instructs a group of children working on the same task at the same time
- Seating groups – where a number of children sit together around a table allowing them to work individually in the company of others
- Collaborative groups – where there is a shared group aim, and work is done together (adapted from Pollard, 2002: 229–30)

The more popular option in English classrooms is to seat children in groups with others of similar ability. This type of grouping is usually used where a teacher has decided to give alternative tasks to groups of children based on their ability. This type of grouping allows children to discuss their individual work with others who have a similar level of understanding and may be valuable for getting to grips with new concepts and ideas. It may not, however, hold the challenges of collaborative group work, or mixed-ability group work, so it is important, if this type of grouping is to be used, to ensure that expectations are appropriate and high for all children.

 ### A Chance to Think

A group of six children, in a class of 7-year-olds, had been identified as having a particular problem with place value. The teaching assistant was asked to play a game with this group to help them to develop their understanding in this area. Each child was given a card with three playing spaces, on which they could place some digit cards.

Several sets of digit cards with numbers from zero to nine were shuffled and placed in the centre. Each child took one card in turn and chose where to put it on her playing spaces. The child with the highest number at the end of three turns was the winner. The children soon learnt to place the higher digits on the hundreds space and the lower digits on the units space. This helped them to understand the importance of the position of the digits in a number. The children enjoyed the game so much that they came back to it later, but this time they tried to get the lowest number that they could.

Partner work, like small-group work, helps to raise children's confidence. Children working in pairs are able to discuss and check their work with a peer before exposing their answer to the teacher or other adult. This allows the children to have more confidence in their response. There are two ways of organizing pairs. The first is where children of similar abilities work closely together towards a common goal, having been given tasks that are suitable for them to tackle as a pair. The second is cooperating as a mixed-ability pair, where peer tutoring can take place. This has the same advantages as the mixed-ability grouping described above, and allows for negotiation, explanation and scaffolding. This approach has to be considered carefully, however, to ensure that the more knowledgeable child does not simply complete the work alone. In both cases personalities need to be paired appropriately.

Fisher (1995: 95) suggested a strategy for paired work, which he called think–pair–share.

1. Students listen while teacher or another poses the questions or problem
2. Students are given time to think of a response
3. Students then pair with a neighbour to discuss their response
4. Finally students share their responses with the whole group

When planning individual work teachers need to realize the extent of each child's capabilities so that needs can be catered for, both during a lesson and in subsequent lessons. Independent work is desirable when undertaking some aspects of the mathematics curriculum, as it promotes a focused and concentrated approach to solving a mathematical question. Repetitive tasks such as the completion of number algorithms are often given to children as individual tasks.

Differentiation

One of the reasons that children may be grouped is to allow the teacher to plan suitable work for a set of children of similar ability. This focused way of planning for individual need is called differentiation and consists of assigning appropriate tasks to individual or groups of children so that each can work at their own level of understanding. Awareness of the possibilities of differentiation should help teachers match tasks appropriately to pupils in the expectation that greater progress will be made (Pollard, 2002). Differentiation for individual children requires the teacher to plan for each child an appropriate, different task or modification of a common task that most closely matches his or her ability.

Differentiation may need to be considered once the nature of the mathematics to be taught and the child groupings have been decided upon (this is certainly the case in English schools, where differentiation for children of different mathematical ability is expected).

As whole-class groupings lend themselves to direct, interactive teaching, differentiation in whole-class lessons would normally be carried out through directed questioning, in other words by directing carefully composed questions at individual children or groups of children. The level of difficulty of the questions will differ from one child to the next and the level of response will also be variable, depending on the ability of the child or children in question. Differentiation can also be channelled through the use of open and closed questions, where higher-ability children would be expected to respond to the more open questions and give reasons for their responses.

 A Chance to Think

A class of 8-year-old children were taking part in a whole-class lesson on fractions. First the teacher revised the work that they had been doing previously and asked several children to colour in halves and quarters of shapes on an overhead transparency. She chose the children who she considered had mastered this concept but who might not yet be ready to answer more difficult questions. As the lesson progressed the teacher asked a child whom she considered to be of higher ability to explain why two quarters was equivalent to one half.

It is the teacher's responsibility to decide upon the most effective way of differentiation for groups or pairs of children. Differentiation can be through task or outcome and can be achieved either in mixed-ability grouping or in same-ability grouping.

Differentiation by task requires that children of similar ability work together. Small groups or pairs can be given different mathematical tasks to do, the content of which is determined by the perceived ability level of the children. Differentiation is probably easier to manage, though, if all groups are given essentially the same task, which is modified for the higher-ability and the lower-ability children. This way, all children feel involved in the lesson and work towards the same or very similar objectives.

 A Chance to Think

A class of 6-year-old children were working on difference. The learning objective for the lesson was the same for all of the children (to be able to work out the difference between two numbers). The low achievers in the class worked with the teaching assistant. They were given some plastic teddies and the teaching assistant posed questions such as, 'What is the difference between two teddies and three teddies?' The children were encouraged to line up the teddies so that they could see the difference in the number in each group.

The group of children who could work confidently with larger numbers worked in pairs and were encouraged to pose (ever more difficult) questions for each other. They recorded their questions and answers in a formal written form, for example 'the difference between 16 and 19 is 3'.

The other chiuldren group worked with the teacher who asked questions such as, 'What is the difference between six and eight?' The children used apparatus of their own choice such as counters, farm animals or play people to help them to work out their answers. They were given a recording sheet on which they were expected to record their answers. It looked like this:

The difference between ☐ and ☐ is ☐.

All of the children were thus working on the same mathematics topic area but at a level that suited them.

Small-group or pair differentiation can also be by outcome. This approach is especially beneficial when the children are engaged in investigative work or problem-solving. It is possible to structure an investigative task so that every child has initial access to the task. All children in a mixed-ability group or pair will be able to begin to tackle the problem at their own level and the mixture of abilities within the group will allow for discussion and explanation to take place between the children about the mathematics involved. When children are to be grouped by ability, the initial stages may be carried out and explored by the lower-ability children and subsequent steps will be explored by the middle-ability children. The higher-ability children will extend their mathematics by tackling the final stages of the investigation where the problem can be explored in different contexts, or where a mathematical generalization is to be arrived at.

A Chance to Think

The children were asked to investigate how many different combinations of clothing can be worn. They were provided with a red T-shirt, a blue T-shirt, a red pair of shorts and a blue pair of shorts. The lower-ability children were expected to try out the clothing combinations and work out the answer. They were then provided with an extra pair of shorts (which were green) and an extra shirt (also green). They were asked to try out the combinations and work in a methodical way. The middle-ability children and high-ability children were expected to begin by drawing the first combinations and then to work logically through the other colour combinations. It was expected that they would be able to make a link between the number of T-shirts and shorts provided with the possible clothing combinations. They were expected to reach some form of generalization. Higher-ability children were expected to be able to extend the task such that they could derive a generalized mathematical equation to allow them to work out the possible number of clothing combinations available with, say, 50 T-shirts and 50 pairs of shorts.

Careful differentiation can go some way to making all children feel motivated, enthusiastic and confident in tackling mathematics.

Enhancing Pupil Participation

Pupil participation is a major element in ensuring that children engage in and enjoy mathematics. Organizing and managing mathematics effectively can not only enhance teaching and learning but also increase the children's enthusiasm, motivation, willingness to learn mathematics and thus their participation in the classroom.

The following techniques will help to ensure that lessons run smoothly and that pupil participation is at its maximum.

- Use a variety of teaching and learning styles and provide contexts for learning that are interesting, familiar and culturally relevant to the children.
- Use a variety of questioning.
- Ensure adequate pace throughout.
- Ensure effective classroom management throughout, including transitions from one activity to another.
- Use a variety of activities.
- Ensure expectations are clear.

Varied Teaching and Learning Styles

Some children work more effectively if provided with a practical or visual approach, whereas others respond better to aural stimuli. Children who have difficulty with formal recording, for example, may benefit and thrive on a practical and oral approach. Some children find that the medium through which the lesson is taught helps to motivate them. For some, the use of ICT to complete a task ensures that there is a greater engagement both with the task and the learning outcomes (Passey *et al.*, 2004).

Different children will benefit from different approaches. You might want to consider certain individuals and then cater for them by differentiation in the task you set, or when you are explaining mathematical ideas you might like to use, say, three different approaches for all the children. When explaining an issue verbally, it is always a good idea to couple it with a visual aid or demonstration that reinforces the message.

 A Chance to Think

A group of Year 1 children were working on subtraction with their teacher. The teacher had some toy cars that she was using to demonstrate the concept of taking away. She asked Tilly and Robert to stand by her. She gave Robert six toy cars and asked Tilly to take two away. She did so and the children decided that Robert now had four left. The teacher then asked the children if anyone could write the question and answer on the small board. Nathan volunteered and he wrote, '6 take away 2 is 4'. Ricky said that he had another shorter way and he wrote '6 − 2 = 4'. The children discussed this way of writing down what they had done. The teacher then chose two more children to demonstrate the taking away with objects and the children took it in turns to write it down on the board. In this way the teacher was explaining the mathematics orally, showing the children the practical application and reinforcing the algorithm by getting the children to write each question and answer on the board. In this way she was using a range of teaching strategies to allow all children to access the style that suited them.

In this connection, we stress again that the context in which the mathematics is presented to the children needs to be appropriate, i.e. interesting, motivating, familiar and culturally relevant (as described in Chapter 3).

It is important for children's continuing motivation and enthusiasm that they are given positive feedback to their work, especially in mathematics which is often seen as difficult and inaccessible. Children must be allowed to celebrate their successes and build on them. Feedback can be given to the children by way of teacher response, test results, their own self-assessment and peer assessment.

 ### A Chance to Think

Class 6 had tackled a mathematical problem in their last lesson. Their teacher decided to show Catherine's work to the rest of the class as part of the next lesson. The children were asked to identify two effective strategies that had been used in this investigation. This not only allowed the class to identify appropriate strategies that they could employ themselves for similar investigations but also gave feedback to Catherine on the success of her investigative skills.

Feedback that will be encouraging to the child will be mainly concerned with the child's own response measured against the learning objective and his or her previous performance, rather than against other pupils. In order for it to be useful, feedback should provide strategies for the improvement of current performance rather than simply highlighting any mistakes that are made.

Fisher (1995) believes that the process of feedback can be summed up in these stages.

- Children should not feel that success is too easy or too difficult to achieve
- They should know what standards to aim at, and the criteria by which to judge their own work and the work of others
- Praise of children's work should be specific and relate to both process and performance, for example 'I like the way you tried with different methods to find the answer, and well done for getting the right answer'

Varied Questioning

Effective questioning is key to engaging and sustaining the children's interest and enthusiasm. To make sure that all children participate in mathematics, teachers commonly use open or closed questioning as a form of differentiation.

Closed questions normally involve the recall of a fact and are therefore useful in ascertaining whether a child has retained information and whether his or her knowledge is sound. Closed questions can be purposefully directed towards individuals or groups and can be appropriately differentiated for individuals.

In this example, the children were all standing by their tables ready for lunch. In order to control the children's exit from the room Sally, the class teacher, asked each one a mathematical question. Each child was allowed to go to lunch on giving the correct answer. As there were children with a range of different mathematical abilities in the class, the teacher planned the questions and directed them at particular children so that all children would be able to give the right answer. The simplest question might be something like 'If I had two marbles and my friend gave me two more how many would I have?' A more complex question might be, 'If there were four of us for tea but only three pizzas, how could I make sure that all of the children had the same amount?'

Open questions can often be answered on different levels and if well framed can allow the children to engage in and demonstrate mathematical thinking and understanding. Open questions are extremely useful if you want to ensure children use higher-order thinking and are able to apply their knowledge to different situations. Again, open questions are a form of differentiation and can be a tool for stretching and extending children's thinking.

A Chance to Think

Bloom's taxonomy of thinking skills defines higher-order thinking skills as evaluation, analysis and synthesis. Examples of questions that require the child to use higher-order thinking skills are, 'Why there are six possible solutions to a problem?' or 'How could we extend the investigation?' Questions that stimulate only lower-order levels of thinking are those that ask for comprehension, application and knowledge, such as 'Explain how you can share this cake between four people?' or 'What do we mean by "add"?'

Well thought-out questions used throughout a lesson will encourage the children to use higher-order thinking, which will in turn enhance their ability to cope with a variety of mathematical problems. The teacher must ensure that all children are involved in the questioning and that open questions are appropriately suited to all abilities and are not just delivered to the mathematically confident children.

When you are planning which questions to put to the children you might like to consider having a variety for which both written and oral responses are expected. This ensures that all children are catered for and that particular needs are individually met.

A Chance to Think

In a class of 9-year-olds Gill, the teacher, had a series of questions prepared to ask the children as part of a mental and oral starter, for example 'If I add two to my number then take away six and multiply by two the answer is four. What is my number?' and 'I am thinking of a number that is six less than eight, is even and can be multiplied by two to make four. What is the number?' Gill asked the first question and the children wrote their answer with a felt-tip pen on small individual whiteboards. They then held their answers up for Gill to see. Gill picked a child who had the correct answer to explain how he or she had worked out the number. As the questions varied in difficulty she was able to pick children to explain from the whole range of mathematical competency within the class.

Pace

Enhanced pupil participation is directly linked to the pace of lessons (Kyriacou, 2001) and the delivery. Too long a delivery and a lack of pace during lessons will allow the children to go off task and lose interest. Explanations are more effective if they are kept brisk and concise, so that a sense of urgency is maintained throughout lessons. At the same time it is important to give the children adequate, but not overgenerous time to carry out any planned activities. It is also essential to set realistic deadlines for the children and to make teacher's expectations clear. One way of keeping children on task and interested is to give them a time by which you expect them to have completed the task and then a 10-minute and 5-minute warning before you ask them to stop.

Ensuring and Maintaining Effective Classroom Management

Good classroom management is essential if children are to learn effectively. Different subjects naturally lend themselves to different working environments and the correct scene must be set and rules and routines well established.

A number of management strategies can be deployed to maintain a purposeful and suitable working environment for the teaching and learning of mathematics. Transitions from one lesson to the next or from one area of the classroom to another need to be carefully managed so that children move or sort out appropriate equipment quickly, sensibly and quietly. If the carpet area is used for whole-class discussion, for example, then the children can be directed to move from the carpet area to their tables in groups, so that not everyone is moving at once.

Transitions from the teaching to the activity part of lessons needs to be well managed and the children need to know exactly how long they have to distribute or clear away resources. Vague instructions and unclear deadlines at the outset of a lesson can set the wrong atmosphere for the remainder of the lesson.

 A Chance to Think

A class of 7-year-old children had been watching and participating in the measuring of a number of items. Jenny, the class teacher, explained the mathematical tasks to be carried out to the children and then sent the children, one group at a time, to get their pencils and rulers from their trays at the side of classroom. She had already put the items that she wanted the children to measure on the tables. Once they had sat down Jenny asked the children to be silent while she explained again the tasks that they were to carry out. This time she also told them that they had 20 minutes to complete their work and that she would let them know how much time they had left as the lesson progressed. After 10 minutes Jenny told the children that they had 10 minutes left and that they should have by now measured at least four of the eight items. She also told the children that if they finished before the time was up they were to find two items in the classroom that they estimated were about as long as 5 cm. With 5 minutes to go Jenny reminded the children that they should nearly be finished and with 1 minute to go she told them to finish the measurement that they were taking and be ready to talk about what they had done. In the last part of the lesson Jenny and the children looked at the items that had been collected with an estimated length of 5 cm, to see how close the estimates had been. In this way Jenny maintained a calm but busy working atmosphere in the classroom. All of the children knew what was expected of them and they all had enough to do to keep them occupied in a worthwhile way.

Children need to be aware of the teacher's expectations before embarking on set tasks. They need to be provided with presentation guidelines and know how much they are expected to achieve within the set time. The teacher needs to keep eye contact with the children and maintain a sense of urgency until they are all settled into the task and then to scan the room constantly to make sure that all children are engaged.

The teacher must provide a variety of appropriate resources (see Chapter 4) that are in good working order, are available for the lesson and are easily accessible by the children. Some teachers prefer to put resources out for each lesson but others like to encourage children's independence by letting them choose their own resources from a maths area or cupboard. If resources are to be placed ready on the tables then they should be out of arm's reach so that full attention can be given to the teacher's exposition or to class interaction.

You should make clear how much working noise you will allow. Some activities will promote more discussion and others will require near silence. Stop the children regularly if the noise level is unacceptable. Remember that even when they need to discuss their thoughts and ideas, this can be done quietly and sensibly.

Using a variety of activities within mathematics lessons will keep the children interested and eager to learn. These activities could include mental and oral work, set tasks, investigational work and problem-solving. Sometimes using alternative approaches, such as giving the children the answer to a word problem and asking them to write the question, or asking them to make up their own mathematical questions either for themselves or for others to answer, can be enjoyable for the children and effective in terms of their mathematical thinking.

Giving clear instructions, explanations and expectations definitely and concisely is essential when working with children in the mathematics classroom. This ensures that the children participate fully, work to their own potential and achieve pleasing and acceptable results. This in turn motivates them and enhances their self-esteem. High standards for all children should be expected and this should be made known to them at the outset of each lesson when instructions are being delivered and reinforced. Self-evaluation – asking them to reflect on the quality and accuracy of their work – is always useful, especially for those children whose work has not met the required standards.

Managing Discussion in Classroom Mathematics

Managing mathematical discussion in lessons is an important aspect of effective teaching and learning. It is vital that children are given the opportunities to talk about mathematics and that teachers provide secure and unthreatening environments in which they can do this.

Talking with the children and allowing them to talk amongst themselves about mathematics is an excellent way to raise competence, confidence and ultimately standards: they learn to express themselves mathematically and become more comfortable with mathematical vocabulary.

Discussion is also a means by which teachers ascertain the extent of children's understanding. Getting children to talk about their thought processes and the reasons for selecting and carrying out various strategies provides valuable insight that wouldn't be evident from marking written work alone. (See Chapter 6 for more on assessment.)

How can you create meaningful discussion about maths?

- Allow time for children to talk amongst themselves about maths
- Allow the children to share their strategies and the reasoning behind their choices
- Scaffold the discussion by careful questioning
- Build thinking time into lessons so that children can consider their answers carefully
- Be positive and encourage responses
- Let the children know that their answers are valued and that we learn through mistakes

In class discussion, teachers must promote turn-taking and respect for the contributions of all of the children. Effective teaching and learning can take place only if the children remain interested and attentive, actively listening and participating fully.

Managing Misconceptions in Mathematics

The misconceptions and mistakes that often arise in mathematics lessons can be used to explain issues further and to reinforce mathematical concepts. It is good to learn from one's mistakes and misconceptions and children need to be encouraged to offer answers and solutions without fear of getting things wrong. They must see that making mistakes is part of the mathematical thinking process and that clearer understanding can come from identification and exploration of their errors. If a teacher encourages children to 'have a go', this helps to provide a positive, safe and secure environment within which children feel more confident to learn mathematics.

 A Chance to Think

What are mistakes?
Mistakes are generally errors that occur through carelessness, where the child has sound understanding of the concept being taught. Once the teacher has prompted the child to check his or her answers or to have another look at the calculations, these errors are usually easily rectified.

Managing mistakes

- Allow children time towards the end of the activity part of the lesson for them to check their work.
- Allow children to check each other's work.
- Ask children to consider the feasibility of their answers and to consider whether they 'look correct'.
- Ask children to estimate answers first, so that they can consider the feasibility of answers more carefully.
- Encourage children not to rush and provide them with minimum times to carry out their work. Tell them that they cannot suggest to the teacher that they have finished their work before the minimum time has elapsed.

What are misconceptions?

Misconceptions are due to lack of understanding or misunderstanding on the children's part. These types of errors are not due to carelessness or being off task, but are much more deep-rooted. Dealing with misconceptions will need careful questioning and further clarification from teachers.

Managing misconceptions

- Always deal with misconceptions as they arise.
- If many children have the same misconception, stop the class and reinforce the issues and concepts again. Keep finding alternative ways of teaching and reinforcing the concepts.
- If individuals have different misconceptions, deal with them discreetly. This may mean stopping the whole class and highlighting a particular problem without indicating who is having the problem. This approach may suit children who lack confidence in mathematics.
- Ensure that suitable, concrete apparatus is available for the children to use. This will help to scaffold understanding where misconceptions occur.
- Use the plenary to go over one or two misconceptions that have arisen during the lesson and share with the children the extent of success of the lesson.
- Share with the children whether they need to carry out more work on the aspects covered, so that they know why concepts are being revisited during subsequent lessons.

Managing Mathematical Play

In reception and nursery classes much of the children's mathematical learning will come through play or playful activity. These two types of play have been separated because they have different starting points and different expected outcomes both in terms of what is learned and how it is learned, which in turn can have an impact on understanding. (See also Chapter 1.)

Children's activities and play in the reception class or the nursery need to be carefully planned. For a background to children's learning in mathematics in the early years and for ideas on planning good-quality mathematical experiences see Montague-Smith (1997).

By 'playful activity' we mean mainly tasks that use commercially produced mathematical materials such as sorting animals and set rings, multilink bricks to make representation of number or pattern, or playing board and other mathematical games. This type of activity is usually teacher-directed and has specific, expected learning outcomes. For example, many board games such as Snakes and Ladders will give children the experience of counting on and counting back, recognition of number order and, if two dice are used, addition. This type of activity allows the children to practise and consolidate mathematical knowledge and skills and allows the teacher to assess these aspects of the child's mathematical work.

Mathematical play is usually child-initiated and may take place in the outdoor play area, role-play area or in 'small worlds' play with, for example, toy cars, roads and play people. This type of activity is very important for children as it affords a context for the mathematics that is being learned and allows them to practise already mastered mathematical ideas in different contexts. Children can also set and solve mathematical problems and develop mathematical ideas

Mathematical play can happen spontaneously but the teacher must also be ready to facilitate it by providing suitable and stimulating materials. The children in Class R, for example, went on a visit to a local garden centre. They were really interested in this and decided with their teacher, Mary, to set up their own garden centre. Mary and the children planned a car park outside with numbered bays for the wheeled toys to park, they made and then sorted the plants into rows in the outside area and they priced the plants. They also set up a garden centre shop with a till for taking the money and a telephone to receive orders, which were written down in the notebook provided. Because of the way in which these areas were set up children were able to write and recognize numbers, sort, match, experience using money, count and make patterns, all in a context that they understood. Mary was able also to assess not only the children's mathematical knowledge and skills but also their mathematical understanding and their ability to solve mathematical problems.

Managing Resources and ICT in the Mathematics Classroom

Using suitable mathematical resources and equipment is an essential part of mathematics lessons and activities (see Chapter 4). They develop and scaffold children's learning and assist those children who need a more concrete approach. Furthermore, mathematical equipment is required in order to carry out many aspects of mathematics. For example, measuring scales are essential for mass work and protractors for angles work.

Children often get excited when apparatus is to be used, so teachers should be adequately prepared and organized. Following simple procedures will ensure that lessons run smoothly, that they are productive and that the apparatus is used safely.

The following will help to minimize fuss and keep children on task:

- Ensure that equipment is ready on table tops before lessons
- Keep the apparatus in the middle of the table tops to ensure that it is out of arm's reach until you are ready for it to be used
- Ensure that children are competent in using the apparatus before asking them to use it independently
- Reinforce the safe use of apparatus and make it quite clear that it is to be looked after and treated appropriately
- Demonstrate how the resources are to be used and how they can help the children with their learning
- Ensure that there are enough resources for every child or group to use
- Insist that all apparatus (including writing materials) is put down and left alone while you are talking to the children
- Give clear deadlines for packing resources away
- Insist that resources are put back into the middle of table tops at the end of lessons and choose one or two children to help with the final tidying away process

We know that ICT can raise the level of pupil attainment when

- It is clearly planned for well-chosen areas of pupil learning
- There is close consultation with class teachers
- It is used over an intensive period (Higgins, 2003)

Like all resources, ICT needs careful management but it has its own particular problems.

Many primary schools have access to ICT suites but this section aims to assist teachers with the management of ICT within the classroom.

It is a mistake to think that ICT is computers and software only. The term 'ICT' encompasses a wide range of equipment. The DfEE (2000) clearly highlights appropriate ICT resources that can be used to support the teaching and learning of mathematics in primary classrooms. They include the following:

- CD ROMs
- Calculators
- Audio cassette tapes
- Computer programmes
- Digital cameras
- Roamers
- TV broadcasts
- The Internet
- Interactive whiteboards
- Video cameras
- Sensory equipment
- Overhead projectors
- Overhead projector calculators

Once teachers have decided to incorporate ICT into lessons, they obviously need to ensure that they know how to operate the equipment competently, that they have had plenty of practice in using it and that they have planned thoroughly in order to prevent mishaps during lessons.

 A Chance to Think

Some tips for successful use of ICT

- To avoid confusion, ensure that OHP calculators match the pocket calculators that the children will be using
- If you allow the children to search the Internet for data, be clear where you expect the children to search and what keywords are appropriate. To prevent any unpleasant surprises, do the search

yourself beforehand and visit the pages on the Internet that you expect the children to visit. Store them as 'favourites' so that you can access them off-line and be sure of what the children are looking at

There are numerous computer programs and CD ROMs now available to support children with mathematics or to reinforce previous learning. The nature of the software you use will dictate how best to use it. It is possible to use a single computer to demonstrate a program to the whole class, but it is essential that it is positioned correctly so that all children can see the screen clearly. If you have acces to a data projector you can enable the whole class to see a projected image of the computer screen clearly. A computer in the classroom can be used additionally for small-group or paired work, when children work on tasks set by the teacher. Of course only a limited number of children can use the computer at any one time or during the course of a lesson. It is advisable not to place more than three children on the computer together. If the group is larger some children will become merely spectators. As in any class arrangement, groupings or pairings need to be carefully thought through and general issues related to single-ability or mixed-ability pairings taken into account. Children need clear instructions for the task so that they understand what you expect them to gain from the ICT experience.

 ### A Chance to Think

You might like to:

- Have a high-achieving child teach a low-achieving child how to use the software
- Have same-ability children working together on the computer
- Have a chain situation where a child teaches one child, and then the new child teaches another child
- Use other adults in the classroom to teach pairs of children at the computer

Think whether it is necessary for all children in the class to have used each piece of computer software. If it is, you will need all your management skills to ensure that all children get through using the computer within a designated time.

Remember that children should all be able to take part in whole-class sessions so that they get access to teaching and discussion.

Managing Other Adults

In primary classrooms there are often other adults present. These might be learning support assistants, teaching assistants, student teachers, parents, carers or guardians. Whoever they are, it is the teachers' responsibility to organize them appropriately. If the adults are to be directly involved with the teaching and learning that is taking place during the mathematics lessons, then they must be briefed beforehand. The teacher needs to make sure that the helpers know what their individual responsibilities are, with whom they are to be working, how much support they are expected to give the children and how the children are expected to present their work. Other adults are valuable assets to any primary classroom and it is essential that teachers treat them with respect, informing them appropriately and working to support them.

Marking, Assessment and Target-setting

Marking is an integral part of the formative assessment process and needs to be managed effectively to ensure that it feeds into future lesson planning. Marking therefore needs to be carried out as soon as possible after the lesson has taken place. However, marking is not the only thing that informs future planning; questioning and observations made during lessons and the feedback received during the plenary or end-of-session discussion can all provide useful information for feeding into future lessons.

Nevertheless, marking plays a significant role in the assessment of work, particularly that of older pupils. It is not always necessary to mark all of the written work that the children produce and you could consider choosing certain groups each day and carry out detailed analysis and marking of their work only. This will help you to manage the marking load over a period of time. The groups that do not receive detailed marking one day may be watched more closely or questioned more thoroughly during the actual lessons so that a clear picture of the whole class's ability is obtained.

Some teachers do prefer to mark all the children's work every day. If you are one of these, then consider marking all their work before planning lessons for the next day. Also consider marking only parts of the work, for example every other question or those which seem more important to analyse.

Once you have done the marking, you need to share it with the children so that they can learn from your advice. You might like to start each lesson by feeding back the main points arising from the children's work. Alternatively, let the children spend the first 5 minutes of the lesson looking at your comments and completing corrections where necessary. Building in time for this ensures that children acknowledge the marking and use this information to develop their understanding.

Formative assessment needs to be carried out regularly so that teachers and children can use the information effectively. It also needs to be carried out and shared quickly, otherwise the knowledge gained will lose its impact and its relevance. Like marking, other assessment processes need to be manageable. You might like to pick small groups of children to work with and observe during each mathematics lesson, so that you can do a focused assessment. The information gained from this and from marking can then be used to set personalized targets for the students. New mathematics targets do not need to be set every day for every pupil, but can be set after a chosen period of time, say after or mid-way through a unit of work.

Targets too need to be shared with the children. Consider having a target sheet in the inside cover of the children's mathematics books so that they can refer to their targets whenever they like and be responsible for working towards them during their mathematics lessons. This also makes it much easier to keep track of children's attainments, as the targets can be signed off as soon as they have been achieved.

Summative assessment, as the name suggests, is the process of summing up a child's understanding and attainment and is used to inform head teachers, parents and future teachers. It is usually carried out after a unit of work has been covered, at the end of the term or at the end of the school year. Summative assessment tends to be more formal and undertaken under test conditions, but as a teacher, unless you are carrying out an externally set test or task, it is up to you to decide how you would like to do it.

Summary

In this chapter we have discussed how effective teaching and learning of mathematics depend on effective organization and management. The teacher has to make sure not only that all the children are able to access the mathematics curriculum but also that each child's needs are met.

This is not an easy task and requires careful thought and planning, a variety of teaching strategies and organizational methods and the consideration of aspects of classroom management.

Planning for lessons and organization of the children will depend on the kind of mathematics that the teacher wants the children to learn, on the planned mathematics activity and on the nature of the class. Planning for essential mathematical play and playful activity, for example, will require a different type of organization from a more formal mathematics lesson. Tailoring the mathematics to children's individual needs, or differentiation, is important in encouraging motivation and developing confidence, enthusiasm and willingness to cooperate and thus participation.

Good classroom management is essential if children are to remain interested and attentive. Pupils should be aware of the working culture that is expected in the classroom as well as understand the nature of the mathematical activity or task they are to undertake. Mathematical discussion and interaction in a secure and unthreatening environment are essential to developing children's learning, assessing their achievements and identifying misconceptions and mistakes.

Part of good classroom management involves the provision of resources. It is essential to provide suitable and interesting resources for mathematical play and mathematics lessons so that children can build up appropriate mathematical understanding. Effective resourcing also includes the use of other adults who can be invaluable in helping with management of the children's learning.

Finally we have discussed the way in which marking, assessment and target-setting can be managed effectively to ensure that they feed into future lesson planning.

Reflective Questions

- In what ways is it possible to group children for mathematics? Can you think of one task or activity where the children's learning would benefit from each kind of grouping?
- What playful mathematical activity could you plan for a class of 10-year-old children?
- How would you involve other adults effectively in the children's mathematical learning?
- How might you manage marking efficiently and how can you ensure that it is meaningful for the children?

REFERENCES AND FURTHER READING

DfEE (2000) 'Using ICT to support Mathematics in the Primary School', Sudbury: DfEE.

Fisher, R. (1995) *Teaching Children to Learn*, Cheltenham: Stanley Thorne.

Higgins S, (2003) 'Does ICT make mathematics teaching more effective?', in Thompson, I. (ed.) *Enhancing Primary Mathematics Teaching*, Maidenhead: Open University Press.

Kyriacou, C. (2001) *Essential Teaching Skills*, (2nd edition), Cheltenham: Nelson Thorne.

Montague-Smith, A. (1997) *Mathematics in Nursery Education*, London: David Fulton.

Passey, D. and Rogers, C. with Machell, J. and McHugh, G. (2004) 'The motivational effect of ICT on pupils', Department of Educational Research, Lancaster University, Research Report RR523.

Pollard, A. (2002) *Reflective Teaching: Effective and Evidence Based Professional Practice*, London: Continuum.

Assessing and Planning Mathematics

INTRODUCTION

One of the important aspects of managing and organizing mathematics lessons is the planning and assessment cycle. We will begin by looking at the links between assessment and planning and how these may vary for children of different ages.

We will consider the issues under the following headings.

- Planning for Assessment and Assessment for Planning
- Planning for Mathematical Learning
- Planning for Recording in Mathematics
- Assessing and Planning ICT in Mathematics
- Assessing and Planning to Avoid or Minimize Misconceptions
- Assessing and Planning for Working with Additional Adults in the Classroom
- Assessing and Planning for Work outside the Classroom
- Assessing and Planning Cross-curricular Work
- Assessing and Planning Out-of–class Work and Homework
- Assessing and Planning for Inclusion
- Assessing through and Planning for Effective Questioning

- Planning the Organization
- Marking, Feedback and Target-setting

Assessing and planning are part of a cyclical process in which the elements are closely bound together. Effective planning relies heavily on assessment evidence, just as carrying out assessment relies on planning. There are of course other non-cyclical elements that impinge on planning and assessment, such as statutory curriculum requirements, which we will mention alongside the more reactive elements involved.

Planning for Assessment and Assessment for Planning

Planning and assessment take place at several levels. This book distinguishes three levels of planning and assessment, each with a different purpose but contributing to effective learning. They are important not least because

Learning is driven by what teachers do in classrooms. Here, teachers have to manage complicated and demanding situations, channelling the personal, emotional and social pressures amongst a group of 30 or so youngsters in order to help them learn now and become better learners in the future. (Black and Wiliam, 1998)

When we talk of planning and assessment in the long term, we mean over a year or more and take into account the continuity and progression of the mathematics curriculum across year groups and throughout the whole school. This type of planning and assessment will be influenced in the first instance by national requirements, which are pre-set and will impinge on the learning and assessment cycle or determine the content of an individual school's planning.

In England, for example, there is the statutory National Curriculum (DfEE, 1999) and the Foundation Stage Curriculum (DfEE, 2001), as well as guidance in the non-statutory National Numeracy Strategy (DfEE, 1999).

In the second place, long-term planning and assessment will be influenced by whole-school issues, such as a school's particular aims and mission statement, which are largely derived from the school's particular needs and aspirations, but also by school policy on issues such as inclusion and multiculturalism. In the case of mathematics, these considerations need to be translated into schemes of work, which will outline the curriculum considered suitable to each year group in a particular school.

It is important that assessment arrangements are included in long-term plans in order to maintain the cycle of planning and assessment. Long-term assessment would be expected to happen at the end of a school year and/or, as in England, at the end of a key stage. It may take the form of a test or series of tests or it may be a summation of the teacher's short- and medium-term assessment records. The most reliable long-term data are probably taken from a mixture of test and teacher assessment, because this gives the children the opportunity to show what they can do in both formal and less formal situations.

The outcomes of long-term assessment may be used for reporting to the child's parents, the school governing body and the child's next teacher. They may also be used for making comparisons between different cohorts of children, to identify targets for the next stage of the children's education and/or to group the children by ability for the next stage of their learning.

In England Statutory Assessment Tests and Tasks are administered at 11 years, constituting summative assessment at the end of the Key Stage 2. In addition national statistics on children's weaknesses in various subject areas are published, which can help teachers to focus on areas that need work, both nationally and in their own school. The Foundation Stage Profile is completed by the end of the Foundation Stage, around the age of 5, requires the teacher to make a judgement about the child's ability to meet a set of criteria, based on observation of the child working and playing in a variety of contexts over a period of time. This Profile, along with the non-statutory tasks and tests for 8- to 10-year-olds can also be used to highlight particular school weaknesses and strengths.

From these long-term schemes of work individual teachers or groups of teachers can develop medium-term plans that are tailored much more closely to their particular class or group of children. The whole-school scheme of work can serve as a guide from which individual medium-term (quarterly or monthly) class plans can be derived. These medium-term plans will rely first on assessment from the previous year's work but should gradually, as the year progresses, become more reactive to the particular class or group.

The National Numeracy Strategy for England (DfEE, 1999) suggests that medium-term plans should comprise termly outlines of units of work and their main teaching objectives and a timetable for teaching them. Medium-term plans are a basis for more detailed short-term plans.

Schools may find it beneficial, in the medium term, to have in place a system of assessments that are undertaken at the end of every term or half term or after short units of work or distinct mathematical topics have been completed. This will allow medium-term plans to be adjusted to accommodate the children's knowledge and understanding. For older children, medium-term assessment will usually take the form of a specially designed task or test to enable the teacher to assess the children in the target group against a key objective or objectives. In reception and nursery, assessment is usually ongoing and does not include the use of tests, although some practitioners may set the children practical mathematical tasks to check progress. Where the assessment is ongoing and informal it is still important to take stock every month or so because such assessment can be very useful for teachers when planning the next stage in children's learning on a particular mathematical theme or topic, as they can refer back to records of previous outcomes.

The National Numeracy Strategy for England suggests that medium-term plans should be evaluated on the basis of short-term assessment of the children. It is suggested that medium-term plans could be annotated to show whether, in general,

Pupils responded well and met the objective in full;
Pupils were responsive but the objective still needs more attention;
An objective was not covered or pupils did not meet it (DfEE, 1999).

It is in the short term, however, that more individual assessment and planning will really come into their own to benefit each child. By short term we mean a week, a short unit of work on a mathematical theme or even a lesson. Assessment opportunities need to be built into these short-term plans so that teachers and practitioners can judge the quality of learning for each individual child and collect information to update their plans. Equally, planning for each lesson in the light of assessment is important, if teaching is to be pitched at the most suitable level to optimize learning.

Short-term assessment is arguably the most important, as this will affect directly what is taught and how a topic is developed and will therefore enhance learning. Teachers need to know about the progress of the children so that work can be adapted to meet their often unpredictable variety of needs (Black and Wiliam, 1998). Short-term assessment is likely to be informal and a normal part of classroom practice. It can take many forms: observation, listening to the children, asking questions and participating in discussion, as well as marking written work, either with the child or later.

Black and Wiliam (1998) claim that there is evidence in the available literature that improving formative assessment and feedback to pupils raises standards, the greatest benefit accruing to (so-called) low attainers.

The evidence from a teacher's or practitioner's daily assessment of the children can be used to fine-tune planning immediately, to adjust a lesson as it goes along or to contribute to the planning of the next lesson. Each part of the lesson can provide opportunities for making assessments. At the beginning of the lesson, for example, teachers often recapitulate and revise earlier work to check the children's understanding before they move on. Based on the children's response, the teacher can make decisions on the most effective way to continue the lesson, for example, s/he can decide whether it is beneficial to reiterate a mathematical idea or whether the children are already secure enough in their understanding. Alternatively the teacher can note the reaction of one or a number of children to feed into future plans.

 ## A Chance to Think

Take the example of Simon and Charlie who had been working on fractions. It was clear that by the end of the lesson they, along with many others in the class, had encountered difficulty with equivalent fractions. The teacher decided to base the mental and oral mathematics starter the next day on this. She provided a bag in which there were large pieces of card with fractions written on them. Four chairs were set at the front of the class labelled with half, a quarter, a third and a sixth. Each child had to take a card from the bag and place it on the chair that had the equivalent fraction. The children discussed each one to see if there was general agreement. They enjoyed the task, which gave them the opportunity to consolidate the previous day's work.

The teacher may choose to work specifically with individuals, pairs or groups of children in order to provide extra teaching, challenge and/ or support. This more child-centred work can enable the teacher to undertake focused assessment of that particular child or group of children.

Often, especially with older children, the teacher will have planned a specific mathematical learning objective or outcome, in which case it is desirable that he or she make written comments about the pupils' understanding of that objective and keep records of these assessments to inform their planning and to feed into their longer-term teacher assessment.

Focused assessment will usually involve the teacher in observation, listening, asking questions and discussing written work. It can give insights into the children's knowledge, mathematical thinking, ways of approaching a task and, more importantly, their understanding, in a way that solitary marking cannot do. This type of assessment can be used immediately, for example to sum up or make further teaching points at the end of a lesson. It can also be recorded with the dual purpose of creating a profile for each child and informing the planning of future lessons.

Younger children especially will need to be assessed primarily by means of observation of their self-initiated play in a familiar context, as this is where they will demonstrate best what they know, understand and are able to do. They can also be assessed through playful activity and even through their idiosyncratic written work (Worthington and Carruthers, 2003).

Where a learning intention has been planned (usually for younger children) the teacher can record a child's response (including what s/he says) on a simple pro forma.

Mathematical profile sheet

Date _____

Name _____

Learning outcome

Where a firm objective has been set (either for playful activity or for more formal mathematical teaching) a teacher working with a group may complete an assessment sheet similar to the example opposite.

Focused Assessment Sheet	
Date _____	
Mathematical Learning Objective _____	

Name	Comment

A plenary or summing up at the end of a lesson can also be used for accurate assessing of the children's understanding, especially if the questions are carefully thought through beforehand, as some questions are much better at yielding assessment information than others. For instance, questions requiring the recall of facts will tell the teacher about the child's mathematical knowledge only, whereas a question about designing and comparing mathematical procedures is more likely to indicate how he or she is thinking and whether the child is able to suggest an efficient strategy. This information can be fed into the next lesson.

Further assessment may take place after the lesson, if the child has produced a recorded outcome from the work. Marking written work, without the presence of the child, gives particular and somewhat limited types of information about the child's response to the work, such as his or her ability to find the correct answer or the process by which the answer was found. It may not give much information about the way a child has worked through a mathematical question or about his or her mathematical thought processes. Marking in this way is usually not immediate, so it can at best only be fed into subsequent lessons.

It is important for children to receive feedback on performance. Traditionally in English schools feedback has mainly been given as grades, comments such as 'good' or 'excellent', gold stars or even 'smiley face' icons. This type of feedback can encourage those who are high achievers but does little for the self-esteem of the rest. It represents a narrow target-led model in which achievement is measured by ability to get the answers right, and engagement in the learning is not encouraged. Pupils who encounter difficulties under this system are led to believe that they lack ability and that they can do little about this (Black and Wiliam, 1998). Instead, teachers need to build a success culture where all work is discussed, problems are acknowledged and worked through and pupils are clear about how they can improve their work.

Feedback to any pupil should be about the particular qualities of his or her work, with advice on what he or she can do to improve, and should avoid comparisons with other pupils. (Black and Wiliam, 1998)

Self-assessment

Children's self-assessment is also a useful tool that can be used to underpin the teacher's short-term assessment. Indeed, Black and Wiliam (1998) believe that, 'self assessment, far from being a luxury, is in fact an essential component of formative assessment'. Sharing objectives at the beginning of a lesson or mathematical topic can increase the children's understanding of what they are expected to learn and the sharing of success criteria may help them to assess their own performance. Children can also be asked to assist with the planning process by their responses to questions from the teacher, such as 'Who thinks they are ready to move on?' or 'Who thinks they need some more practice with this?'

Self-assessment allows children to think through the knowledge and understanding that they have gained in a lesson or topic and gives them an opportunity to consolidate their learning.

Children are often much better at assessing their own progress than they are given credit for and often too have an understanding of the roles of the adults who help them.

 A Chance to Think

A study by Muschamp (in Pollard and Bourne, 1994: 230) revealed just how astute children's comments could be.

John, aged 7, said 'My best subject is maths. I know all my tables. My Granddad teaches me.' Milena, also aged 7, said, however, 'I am not very good at maths. I find it hard. I'll make mistakes and the teacher will tell me to do it again.'

As we have seen, assessment can help to give an accurate picture of the current mathematical understanding of the children. Although many teachers plan lessons well ahead, they should be flexible and able to change their planning in the light of assessment. It might, for example, be necessary to slow down to accommodate more work on a particular aspect of mathematics or, if the children seem to have understood an idea more quickly than expected, to accelerate, enabling the children to build on their strengths. Many teachers plan outline mathematics lessons for the week, adding detail daily, which allows for assessment and amendments as appropriate.

 ## A Chance to Think

Harvinda, the Year 6 class teacher, had decided to look at measuring and calculating area and perimeter of rectangular shapes and compounds of rectangular shapes. She planned a sequence of five lessons over one week. She decided to look at perimeters on day one. She knew that they had done a great deal of work on this in Year 5 and thought that they would probably be comfortable with this concept. The children would then look at calculating area on days two and three. On days four and five she planned to look at area and perimeter together in order to help the children understand the relationships between the two. As soon as day one, however, she realized that the children did not understand the notion of perimeter and many children were trying to multiply the lengths and breadths of the shapes that they had been given rather than adding them. She decided therefore to spend day two again working on perimeter, but in more practical contexts. The children were all taken out into the playground where they measured the perimeter of the play area and the various school buildings. This helped the children to embed the concept of perimeter more securely.

Planning for Mathematical Learning

Teachers planning for mathematics must consider the age and stage of the children and what they would like the children to achieve.

It is desirable that the youngest children access most of their mathematics through play or playful activity, and planning will be through intended learning outcomes. Older children are likely to have more formal mathematics lessons with pre-set learning objectives.

Mathematics experienced during child-initiated play can be a particularly powerful learning experience for the children as it gives them opportunities to learn and practise their mathematics in a context that they have chosen themselves, to interact with each other and sometimes with a more knowledgeable adult and to connect different areas of mathematics together. One disadvantage of this type of activity is that the teacher may have little control over the mathematical ideas in which the children engage. The way round this is for the teacher to provide resources and ideas. In England, unlike most of the rest of Europe, this type of play is usually restricted to the nursery and reception classes (children aged 3 to 5). It is worth thinking about the value of giving older children the opportunity to engage in this type of play.

 A Chance to Think

In an English reception class (children aged 4 to 5) the teacher had planned mathematical activities to encourage counting and matching. One such activity was in an area set out as a 'home corner'. There were items that might be found in any typical home including cutlery, crockery, tablecloths, a phone and paper. The four children playing there covered the table with a cloth, set chairs around the table for the two dolls, the teddy and the toy rabbit and put one doll or soft toy on each chair. They counted out plates, cups, knives and forks and put one in front of each doll. They arranged the food on plates and set about giving food and drinks to the dolls and soft toys. There was a wealth of mathematics in this activity including area, sorting, matching, counting, sharing and pattern-making.

Adults working in the classroom can sometimes join in with the children's play so that mathematical ideas are built on. They should not, however, inhibit or hijack the children's chosen activities or skew their play to conform to the teacher's expected outcome rather than the pupils' spontaneous ideas.

Some children were playing in a shop that had been set up in a corner of the classroom. The teacher decided to go to the shop as a customer and buy a toy, itself a mathematical activity. She noticed that the children were counting out a random mixture of coins. She suggested that perhaps the items in the shop should have prices on them. She and the children decided together that the shop should be a 'pound' shop with everything costing £1, £2 or £3 and together they set about making price labels. The children were encouraged to count out the correct number of pound coins for their purchases. They went on playing in this way when the teacher left the shop, but now they were carefully counting the correct number of pound coins for their purchases.

When teachers are planning for self-initiated mathematical play they need to have a clear idea which mathematical areas are likely to be included in the play, so as to allow the opportunities and outcomes to be recorded and to ensure coverage of important mathematical concepts and ideas can be ensured in the longer term.

Planning for self initiated mathematical play is likely to follow a format like the one shown on the next page.

Only three play areas have been shown here but other areas or activities that the children might choose could be added to this, for example sand, water, art and building blocks.

Playful mathematical activity can also be useful in developing children's mathematical understanding at any age. Planning here might include teacher-directed activity with structured or unstructured resources including such things as multi-link, small plastic coloured bears in different sizes, board or card games, dominoes or computer games. This type of play, as opposed to self-initiated play, will have different outcomes for the child. Playful mathematical activities are usually enjoyable for the children and are have the advantage of being focused on the teacher's learning intentions. This allows the teacher to control which mathematical ideas the children are introduced to and which mathematical concepts are practised (for example counting or matching). It has the disadvantage, though, of tending to be narrower in scope and range than self-initiated play, usually restricting the learner to one mathematical concept at a time. As the child is not in control, interest may also be more difficult to maintain, especially that of the younger child, who may not be as deeply involved.

It is important to try to get the correct balance between child-initiated play and adult-directed playful activity, as well as between adult intervention

Self-initiated play

Week beginning _____ (e.g. 15 September) _____

Topic area _____ (e.g. the garden centre) _____

Implications from previous work
Many children can now count to 10 and understand one-to-one correspondence

---

Areas of possible mathematics coverage
Practice and consolidation of counting and the opportunity to engage in some simple addition

---

Area of activity Indoor role-play area	*Possible learning outcomes* 1. Use pennies to buy small items (simple addition) 2. 3.
	Resources 1. Items to buy – seed packs, garden tools, flower pots, etc. 2. One-penny coins 3. Till 4.
	Assessment Who will be observed and on which day.
Outdoor play area	*Possible learning outcomes*
	Resources
	Assessment
'Small worlds' play	*Possible learning outcomes*
	Resources
	Assessment

and allowing the children the space and freedom to play on their own. The balance will change with age but all children need time for child-initiated play and the younger they are, the more time they need for this.

Later on, children will inevitably have more paper-based mathematical activity but as many young children learn best in a practical and active way it is important even here to plan for plenty of opportunity for practical work and interaction with resources, other children and adults (see Chapters 1 and 2 for the importance of practical and contextualized mathematics). Discussion is also an effective tool in children's learning of mathematics, as children rehearse and practise the language and vocabulary of mathematics. An effective lesson plan for children who are older might look like this:

Mathematics Implications of previous learning Possible misconceptions
Intended learning outcomes (Foundation Stage) or learning objectives: <ul><li>Mental and oral work</li><li>Main activity</li></ul>
National Curriculum reference or Early Learning Goal reference
Key vocabulary (for mental and oral work and for main activity)
Mental and oral work: e.g. <ul><li>Activity</li><li>Differentiated key questions</li></ul> *Main activity:* e.g. <ul><li>Teaching points and differentiated key questions for direct, interactive whole-class/group teaching</li><li>Activities and organization/grouping</li><li>Teacher focus</li><li>LSA focus</li></ul>
Plenary: e.g. Teaching points and key questions to include some of the following: <ul><li>Consolidation of LO in same context</li><li>Use and application of LO in different context</li><li>Possible misconceptions</li><li>Assessment questions</li><li>Extension</li><li>(Out of class/homework)</li></ul>
Resources (including ICT if appropriate)
Assessment: e.g. What? (should be linked to the learning objectives) How? Who?

As we have said, such outline plans for mathematics must be refined further to take account of previous learning and to build in opportunities for children to demonstrate their learning.

Planning for Recording in Mathematics

Recording mathematics in a formal way is difficult, especially at first, and if children are asked to do this too soon it may discourage them from enjoying their mathematics and prevent them from establishing positive attitudes to the subject. As they mature, however, pupils need to develop the ability to carry out and record their mathematics in an independent, logical and systematic way. You can encourage them by giving them the space and opportunity to work out their own ways of recording and to talk about these with other children and adults so as to refine their own ideas. Discussing a child's idiosyncratic recording with him or her demonstrates the child's mathematical thinking and thus presents a good assessment opportunity (Worthington and Carruthers, 2003).

In some English pre-schools over-use of worksheets has meant that children have not had the opportunity to develop their own recording methods, which in turn means that they are denied the opportunity to demonstrate their understanding. You can facilitate their recording by supplying appropriate resources. This is not to suggest that children be given a recording pro forma on which to write, more that consideration should be given to helping the children to demonstrate what they know. The provision of counters or a number line, for example, could influence the way in which a mathematical task is approached and recorded. Similarly the provision of different types of paper can lead to different types of written response.

 A Chance to Think

Some 8-year-old children were exploring the flora present in different areas of their school playing field. Those who were given plain paper drew what they had seen and made tally charts and those that were also given squared paper used it to present block graphs. Both had collected the data but only those who had constructed the graph were easily able to make inferences from the data collected.

Assessing and Planning ICT within Mathematics

ICT can be a powerful means of enhancing the learning of mathematics. Many children enjoy using computers and other ICT resources in the classroom and at home. Unfortunately the ravages of school life and the vagaries of electronic gadgetry mean that the ICT equipment is not always reliable and it is therefore important for the teacher to check, well in advance of the lesson, that all is working.

ICT should be used in mathematics lessons only if it will enhance the learning of a particular objective that is thought to be appropriate for the children at the time. In order to plan appropriately teachers need to keep abreast of the software and hardware available to them. It can be beneficial to develop a list on which teachers can enter new websites or other sources of information that may be of use to other teachers in the school. It is also a good idea to list available software under the resources section of the school mathematics scheme of work.

In the UK the Association of Teachers of Mathematics (ATM) and *The Times Educational Supplement (TES)* recommend various items of software as well as listing websites recommended by teachers.

The nature of the ICT resources that are available will often dictate how they can be used in the classroom. Time will need to be planned into lessons for teaching the children how to use the mathematical software so that they can make the most of it. Sometimes children will need to work individually, sometimes in groups and sometimes as a whole class.

Self-assessment is often possible with ICT-based resources, allowing children to receive instant feedback and correct their mistakes. Some computer programs record assessment data for the children as they log on and use specific programs. Teachers can look at this assessment data at a later time to assist with their general assessment. Other programs, however, provide little opportunity for teachers to analyse children's thoughts and understanding, unless they are working with the children and are able to observe their interaction. In such cases children could be asked to draw or write about their reactions to the program or to note down any scores that are given.

One fairly new and very helpful aspect of ICT is interactive whiteboards. These allow a large group or whole class of children to interact with ICT, with the teacher and with one another. They are also good for discussions, as all contributions can be seen on the screen by the children.

In the UK the DfES Numeracy website has some helpful Interactive Whiteboard programs at www.standards.dfes.gov.uk/numeracy/publications. In addition National Whiteboard Network's website is specifically dedicated to supporting interactive whiteboards in numeracy, at www.nwnet.org.uk.

Assessing and Planning to Avoid or Minimize Misconceptions

When planning, teachers need to be aware of potential misconceptions surrounding mathematical topics that children might develop, or may already have. Knowing where such misconceptions may arise will help the teacher find ways of avoiding them or of minimizing their effect.

In order to be aware of potential troublespots, teachers need a good level of subject knowledge, meaning not just knowledge of the subject content but also pedagogical knowledge about how children learn mathematics and, in particular, aspects that many find difficult. For example, children often measure with a ruler from the end of the plastic instead of from the zero mark on the scale. If a teacher knows that this is likely to be a problem, he or she can emphasize to the children where to place the ruler in order to measure accurately.

It is important that teachers diagnose children's mistakes in their mathematics and analyse the cause. A mistake may be a one-off careless slip or it may reveal a lack of understanding. Misconceptions can be identified by observing and/or talking to the child or by looking at a child's written work. Talking through a mathematical problem with a child allows the child to explain his or her thinking. This may show up an error or misconception and allows the teacher to act immediately to help the child understand how and where an error has been made.

 A Chance to Think

Here is an example of a common procedural mistake in subtraction using decomposition. The child set out her work like this.

```
  2 4 3
 −1 5 9
 ─────
    1 6
```

Can you see where the problem lies?

Clearly, once a misconception has been identified it is important the child receives help. Usually repeating an explanation or activity is not effective, the teacher will probably have to explain the procedure or concept in a different way, provide appropriate resources to help the child or create the opportunity for the child to clarify his or her thoughts, perhaps by asking questions. If the misconception is noticed within the lesson it can be dealt with at the time. If the misconception is discovered on marking the work then the teacher should set aside time to deal with the problem the next day.

Misconceptions can be a useful starting point for teaching, but children's errors need to be handled sensitively because pointing them out publicly can lead to low self-esteem and demotivation. A supportive classroom ethos, though, can be built in which children can be taught to see that mistakes are valuable learning opportunities. Interaction between the teacher and the children is of course important but remember, while planning, that it is also helpful for children to explain mathematical processes and concepts to one another, a process known as peer tutoring. This helps the more knowledgeable children consolidate their own learning by having to break down the recently mastered mathematics into small steps and the less knowledgeable children benefit as the explanation comes from someone who has just mastered a mathematical topic and therefore may better understand the difficulties.

Assessing and Planning for Working with Additional Adults in the Classroom for Mathematics

Additional adults can be extremely valuable both to aid the children's learning in mathematics and to collect data for assessment. To get maximum benefit from adults working in the classroom their input has to be well planned and coordinated. Additional adults may include Teaching Assistants (TAs), Learning Support Assistants (LSAs), Classroom Assistants (CAs), older pupils, trainee teachers, students on child-care courses, secondary school students on work experience, parent helpers, helping governors and other volunteers.

In order to maximize the children's learning, any additional adults must be made aware of the purpose of any mathematical activity that is to be undertaken and recognize the mathematical learning that the teacher expects to take place. It would be ideal if additional adults could be involved in planning the mathematics work and activities, as this would give them a better understanding of the purpose of the work and the expected outcomes. This is not usually realistic, though, except in the case of trainee teachers who are expected to work alongside the teacher both inside and outside school hours for planning and assessment. Volunteers are not usually available before or after school and paid teaching assistants are usually contracted to work only during school hours. This means that the teacher will need to find alternative ways of briefing these adults and working closely with them.

In whole-class teaching situations, additional adults can demonstrate appropriate types of interaction or they can model the types of responses that the teacher expects. If the teacher asks for examples of mathematical strategies to complete a problem, the teaching assistant might provide a strategy, so as to encourage the class to contribute alternatives. Or an additional adult might be asked to write down the responses of a few given children or note those children who do not take part as this can contribute to assessment.

Working with small groups or individual children, additional adults can help by repeating or reading questions, reminding children of the teacher's instructions or earlier explanation, scribing for those who have writing difficulties or operating ICT equipment. Adults can also take part in group or paired discussion using key vocabulary and help the children by encouraging or prompting.

The teacher's planning should make it possible for the adult to concentrate on helping the children to understand, rather than just helping them to complete the work. Therefore the adult needs to be told what the activity is, how to do it, what the children are expected to do and what the children should do once they have finished. It is also useful if they have access to a list of the main words that the children are expected to know, understand and use and a list of key questions to ask the children. The adult should also have some mechanism for feeding back to the teacher and to the children at the end of a lesson.

If the teacher has no time to talk the adult helper through the mathematical activity then the provision of a pro forma might be helpful.

It is beneficial for both the children and the adults if assistants who are in the classroom regularly, such as TAs, work with a variety of children over time.

Date _____

Please work with _____

Learning intention(s)

Activity

Key vocabulary

Key questions

If the children finish early, please

I would be grateful for feedback about how well the children managed to achieve the learning intention.

Names	Comments

Any other comments

Thank you

Naz, a TA in a class of 9-year-old children in England, was always directed by the class teacher, Mary, to work with the group of children who usually had some problems with understanding mathematical ideas. The group became over-reliant on Naz which reduced their independence and Naz was often left feeling frustrated and unchallenged. Mary rarely, if ever, worked with this group. This was a pity, as they would have benefited greatly from her expert input. Naz would have enjoyed the opportunity occasionally to work with other groups of children as she felt that she could have helped them to consolidate their understanding and provided them with extra challenges.

It should also be recognized that additional adults will come from diferent backgrounds and their level of mathematical experience, their skill in sharing it and their confidence in their subject knowledge will vary considerably.

Assessing and Planning for Work outside the Classroom and Assessing and Planning Cross-curricular Work

Mathematics in school will often be taught as a discrete subject, but of course children do not experience life as separate subjects, so the context of mathematical learning needs to be made real for the child. One way of doing this is to adopt a cross-curricular approach or identify cross-curricular links, giving opportunities for learning and using mathematics within planned themes or topics.

 A Chance to Think

A class of 8-year-olds were exploring the theme of gardens and opportunities for mathematics were identified in: sorting and counting seeds; growing plants and recording their growth including measuring; and visiting a local garden centre where the children bought seeds and calculated totals and change.

Even in a school that does not work to themes or topics it is still possible to build cross-curricular links. Some examples of links with other subjects are suggested in the table opposite but this is clearly not an exhaustive list.

Subject	Links with mathematics
English	Use stories and poems for starting points for mathematics work as well as English.
	Provide opportunities for children to develop their speaking and listening skills through small-group and paired discussion in mathematics.
Science	Measuring.
	Using scientific data to generate data-handling activities in mathematics.
ICT	Using mathematics CD ROMs, Internet sites and other ICT devices such as floor turtles.
	Use of spreadsheets.
Design and Technology	Accurate drawing and measuring.
History	Sequencing.
	Handling data.
	Working out 'how long ago' or 'how long between'. History of mathematics and mathematicians.
Geography	Handling data.
	Maps.
	Distances.
	Times.
	Mathematics in other countries and languages.
Religious Education	Patterns and symbols.
Physical Education	Times.
	Distances.
	Speeds.
	Scores.
	Shapes, patterns and symmetry.
Music	Patterns and rhythms.
	Songs for mathematics e.g. 'Ten Green Bottles'.
Art	Patterns, shape and symmetry.
	Paper folding and origami.
Modern Foreign Languages	Counting – many mental and oral starter games can be played in a different language.
	Dates and telling the time.

It is always appropriate to point out the links to the children and to encourage them to make connections between mathematics and other subjects and within mathematics itself. These opportunities may occur in mathematics lessons or in lessons for other subjects.

The youngest children, who learn mainly through play, are likely to learn mathematics in a cross-curricular way by playing with many different resources in the nursery or school environment, including the role-play area, the construction toys, in art and craft activities through songs and playing musical instruments, playing with balls, bean bags and other physical education resources, and playing inside and out of doors.

The Curriculum Guidance for the Foundation Stage (DfES, 2000) recommends that many children's activities, across all areas of learning should take place outdoors. Here mathematical opportunities for young children might include playing with ride-on and push-along toys, role play, building with large blocks, water play and sand play. For all children, including older ones, mathematics can be experienced in real and relevant contexts outside the classroom, in the school grounds or even further afield, an environment that is often underused.

In or near the school grounds children can look for patterns in nature, both on a macro level, such as changing seasons, and on a micro level, such as leaf patterns. They can also look for man-made patterns such as bricks in a wall or the placing of street lights. Children may also find objects or instances that can be counted, such as numbers of woodlice under a stone or how many times they hear a car pass. They can also look for shapes, take measurements and collect data.

 A Chance to Think

Fibonacci's numbers can be seen in natural objects such as pine cones, flower petals and flower seed heads. The University of Surrey has an informative website suggesting investigations with such objects, at http://www.mcs.surrey.ac.uk/personal/R.Knott/Fibonacci/fib.html.

Away from school, visits to local shops, a supermarket, a garden centre, a farm or to less obvious venues, such as places of worship and sites of historic interest, will all provide opportunities for looking at pattern, symmetry, shape, measuring, counting, calculating and data handling. As with any visit away from school, you must undertake a risk assessment in advance and adhere to current health and safety guidelines.

A class of 7-year-olds made a visit to a local baker. They were able to measure ingredients for the dough, see the dough rise, watch as the risen dough was weighed and shaped into rolls and discuss oven temperature and timing with the baker. They watched the cooked rolls being packaged and visited the shop to buy their own roll, which they later ate for lunch.

Much work of this kind would need to be assessed by observing and listening to children as they use mathematical language and demonstrate their understanding through discussion. Older children may be able to record some of their own work in situ and there may also be some opportunities for recorded outcomes on return to the classroom.

Assessing and Planning for Out-of-class Work and Homework

We know that children often have difficulties linking mathematical work that is done in school to the mathematical activity that goes on outside it (see Chapter 1). The most effective out-of-class work and homework will therefore try to make use of the home–school link. Thorough planning is again the watchword.

 A Chance to Think

A class of 10-year-old children had been working on percentages in mathematics and nutrition in science. They were asked by their teacher to look on three tins or packets of food at home and to work out from the nutrition information on the label the percentage of each food type that was present. This activity gave a realistic context to their work and helped them to link school mathematics not only with home but also with science.

Naturally it is imperative in this context first to consider whether any necessary resources are likely to be available at home. Homework can be set for the children to do completely independently, but involving adults or older siblings at home can lead to a richer experience that can give children an insight into the uses of mathematics outside school, an opportunity to think through what they have learned by explaining to an interested other and the opportunity to practise vocabulary. In this case, the adults at home must be kept informed about the ways in which the children are learning mathematics so the children find reinforcement rather than confusion, which can happen if they are introduced to alternative methods, or even demotivation if the adults at home are unable to beome involved.

 A Chance to Think

Jenny, aged 5, had been sorting coins in school. Her teacher sent home a note indicating that the children in the class had been working on coin recognition and suggesting it would be helpful if they could sort the coins in an adult's purse or wallet. Jenny's mother was keen to do this as it enabled her to understand what was going on in school and to be involved in what Jenny was working on. Regrettably, not all parents react so positively to the invitation to be involved in their children's learning.

It is important that teachers follow up on any homework that is set in school, for several reasons. Homework can give the children valuable practice and allow for consolidation of the mathematics learned that day. Equally, homework completed the day before can be followed up in school, allowing the children to discuss the mathematics that they have undertaken at home. Children also need to know that any mathematics they do outside school is important and that their efforts are valued. The provision of homework can also emphasize the important links between home and school.

Assessing and Planning for Inclusion

Children have a range of different cultural needs, physical needs and emotional needs, along with a variety of learning styles, for example some children are more visual learners than others. These needs should be considered at the planning stage to ensure that the mathematics curriculum is accessible to all and that all children are catered for by, for example, using stimulating visual aids, explaining clearly, encouraging discussion, creating opportunities for children to record in their own way and providing interesting activities. Children's preferences, competences, confidence and rate of progression also vary greatly and change over time.

Gifted and talented children should not be forgotten. They need to be challenged and so planning for them might include additional open-ended investigational activities and problem-solving at a higher level than for the rest of the class. (See Chapter 7 for more on special educational needs.)

Assessing through and Planning for Effective Questioning

Questioning can be a powerful way of helping children forward in their learning and of assessing their knowledge and understanding. With key questions and prompts, planned ahead, children can be encouraged to think through mathematical ideas, concepts and processes. Good questioning also facilitates assessment of the children's understanding of the teacher's learning intention.

Children should also be encouraged to ask questions of each other and the teacher and to engage in mathematical discussion, so that they can use mathematical vocabulary and explain concepts, which in turn helps to crystallize their understanding. Similarly, mathematical discussion helps the teacher to understand better the children's thinking, which can be used to inform assessment.

Open questions encourage discussion and challenge children's thinking. When devising the questions it is useful to identify the different kinds of thinking and/or responses that are hoped for, for example recalling facts or processes identifying facts, applying reasoning, hypothesizing and predicting, designing and comparing procedure.

Planning the Organization

The organization of the children, resources, space and additional adult(s) is a key consideration in promoting effective teaching and learning within mathematics. Although this is dealt with in depth in Chapter 5 it is relevant to say here that different mathematics lessons will require different organization, depending on the learning intention, the age and maturity of the children, resources available, including adult support, and prior assessment.

Marking, Feedback and Target-setting

The many and varied stakeholders in education require feedback about the mathematical work and attainment of the children. They include the head teacher, other teachers in the school, parents, governors, the local education authority, school inspectors and others who have influence on the education of the young. Most importantly, though, as we have already mentioned, the children will need feedback themselves. This is the aspect that will be discussed here.

Much of the feedback that children receive from their mathematical work will be in the form of careful assessment by the teacher. It is probably best for the children's learning if their efforts are marked either in their presence or as soon as possible after the work is completed so that feedback can be given promptly. Marking work in progress is advantageous as the child is able to discuss the work with the teacher and act upon feedback and advice immediately. It can also mean that a child does not practise a misconception or error. With the youngest children immediate feedback from the teacher is even more essential as much of their work is likely to be of a practical and oral nature and may not have recorded outcomes.

It is, of course, not always possible in a busy classroom to mark and give immediate feedback to all of the children all of the time and it may be that different groups of children have the opportunity each day. To overcome this problem some teachers may use the plenary or summary of the lesson to enable the children to self-mark their work. This information plus observation of the children's response allows the teacher to provide some general feedback to the whole class, which may include extra input or discussion on more difficult aspects or general problems the children have encountered.

At times work will be marked without the presence of the child, either because the teacher chooses to do it that way or because it is more appropriate, for example in test situations. In all circumstances, it is vital to keep in mind the purpose of the marking. If marking is to be helpful in terms of learning for the child, then feedback that identifies the features that need to be thought about is the most useful. This could take the form of a written or verbal discussion between the child and the teacher. If, on the other hand, marking is to satisfy one of the more remote stakeholders such as the local authority then it is more likely to take a numerical form such as the awarding of a percentage mark.

From careful marking and assessment targets can be set for individual children. Many teachers find that target-setting in mathematics is more manageable when children with similar profiles are grouped together and targets are set for those groups. To be used effectively, targets need to be closely related to what the children are already able to do, they should be short-term and they should have clear success criteria. Involving children in the target-setting process throughout their primary school years encourages them to take responsibility for their own learning. It also provides opportunity to celebrate the children's work.

Summary

In this chapter we have looked at the issues of planning and assessment in mathematics and how they are interwoven. We have seen how effective planning that promotes effective learning is dependent on effective assessment, and that assessment also has to be planned for. For individual children, being aware of the learning intentions planned, understanding what they need to learn and being part of the assessment process, can make the learning experience much more motivating and successful.

Reflective Questions

- Why is the planning assessment cycle so important in the classroom?
- What are the differences between planning for Foundation Stage children (aged 3 to 5) and planning for primary school children (aged 5 to 11)?
- How might you keep assessment and target-setting manageable in the classroom?
- How might you go about involving children in assessing their own mathematical learning?

REFERENCES AND FURTHER READING

Black, P. and Wiliam, D. (1998) 'Inside the Black Box',
www.kcl.ac.uk/depsta/education/publications/blackbox.html

DfEE (1999) *The National Curriculum*, London: DfEE.

DfEE (1999) *The National Numeracy Strategy*, London: DfEE.

DfEE (2001) *The Foundation Stage Curriculum*, London: DfEE.

Muschamp, Y. (1994) 'Target setting with young children', cited in Pollard, A. and
Bourne, J. (eds) *Teaching and Learning in the Primary School*, London: Routledge Falmer.

Worthington, M. and Carruthers, E. (2003) *Children's Mathematics: Making Marks,
Making Meaning*, London: Paul Chapman.

www.mcs.surrey.ac.uk/personal/R.Knott/fibonacci/fib.html

www.nwnet.org.uk

www.standards.dfes.gov.uk/numeracy/publications

Equal Opportunities and Special Educational Needs in Mathematics

INTRODUCTION

This chapter will explore some of the issues of ensuring equal opportunities for all children in the learning of mathematics. It looks at the needs of those children in mainstream schools or in pre-school settings who have some difficulty accessing the mathematics curriculum because they find it demanding, are excluded in some way or are ahead of their peer group mathematically and need to be challenged.

We will, therefore, look at:

- Children with special educational needs in mathematics
- Teachers' responses to special educational needs in mathematics
- Planning for children with special educational needs
- Teaching and learning
- Dyscalculia
- Reading and language difficulties
- Pupils with sensory or physical disabilities

- Building self-esteem and enthusiasm
- Using other adults

Planning is, as always, the key to ensuring equality of access. All classes and settings in a school will, of course, have a different combination of children. Most classes will be mixed and will have pupils from different social and cultural backgrounds. Many classes will also include children with special educational needs, pupils with disabilities, pupils of different ethnic groups including travellers, refugees and asylum seekers and/or children from diverse linguistic backgrounds. The challenge for teachers in including all these children in the mathematics that takes place in the class is to overcome barriers to learning by providing the learning environment or special tools that they may need and to match the mathematics curriculum to children's individual needs, usually by differentiation.

Children with Special Educational Needs in Mathematics

For the purposes of this chapter children with special educational needs are defined as those who, for whatever reason, have specific needs in mathematics and to whom special consideration needs to be given.

The code of practice for England defines children with special educational needs as those who have a learning difficulty, which calls for special provision to be made for them.

Children have a learning difficulty if they:

a) *have significantly greater difficulty in learning than the majority of children the same age; or*

b) *have a disability which prevents or hinders them for making use of educational facilities of a kind generally provided for children of the same age in schools within an area of the local education authority; or*

c) *are under the age of compulsory school age and fall within the definition at (a) or (b) above or would do so if special provision were not made for them.* (DfES, 2001: 6)

There are two main groups for whom special provision needs to be made within the classroom or pre-school setting. They are the children who find mathematics demanding or even inaccessible and those who find the mathematics curriculum undemanding.

Children who struggle with mathematics, whose progress gives cause for concern or who underachieve are often described in the literature as low attainers (Haylock, 1991). Difficulties may be physical, sensory, behavioural, emotional or neurological, or may stem from a legacy of poor learning, which affects current progress. Some of these children may have particular problems with mathematics, which are often but not always associated with literacy problems (DfEE, 1999).

There is some concern about low attainment in mathematics in the UK and as a consequence of this several initiatives have been put in place. For example, there are numeracy booster classes in Year 6 which are designed to give intensive and targeted support to children who need it, so that they gain the expected Level 4 in Key Stage assessments; and 'springboard', which is to designed to boost the attainment of Year 3, 4 and 5 children who gained a good Level 2 in their end of Key Stage 1 assessments at age 7. These initiatives give only short-term support and are aimed at helping children to achieve higher results at the end of Key Stage 2. They should not be seen as a substitute for creating a climate where ongoing support gives children the opportunity to develop firm and lasting mathematical knowledge and understanding

Pupils who are ahead of their expected chronological age group or for whom mathematics is not challenging enough to meet their needs are often known as gifted and able. As the National Numeracy Strategy for England (DfEE, 1999) points out,

mathematically able pupils are among all ethnic and socio-economic groups. They typically:

- *Grasp new materials quickly;*
- *Are prepared to approach problems from different directions and persist in finding solutions;*
- *Generalise patterns and relationships;*
- *Use mathematical symbols confidently;*
- *Develop concise logical arguments.*

All children need consideration and the way in which the teacher responds to the pupils in both of these groups will have a considerable impact on their learning.

Teachers' Responses to SEN in Mathematics

There are a number of reasons why some children underachieve in mathematics: cultural, emotional, physical or medical, or related to the children's previous experiences. Some of the problems that children encounter may arise because of a mismatch between home and school experience as described in Chapter 1. It should be remembered that children with special educational needs are not essentially different from other children and they progress better if the teacher is able to emphasize the links between what the children know and what they are to learn rather than emphasizing what they do not understand.

Teachers have a responsibility to ensure that all pupils can access the mathematics curriculum and that every child is given the opportunity to experience success in learning and achieve as high a standard as possible. This means meeting the specific needs of individuals and groups of pupils. Certainly, specific groups of children have more difficulty accessing the curriculum than others. They include children with English as an additional language (EAL), those whose home background is culturally different from that of the classroom, those who have physical or sensory disabilities, those who find mathematics difficult and demanding and those who are more able in mathematics than their peers.

The English National Curriculum sets out three principles that are considered to be essential in developing a more inclusive curriculum. These are:

A. Setting suitable learning challenges
B. Responding to pupils' diverse learning needs
C. Overcoming potential barriers to learning and assessment for individuals and groups of pupils (DfEE, 1999)

Because all children need to be able to access a mathematics curriculum that is suitable for them, teachers must be reactive to individuals' needs and plan a curriculum accordingly. This does not mean that they have to provide separate work for each child, as individual needs do not necessarily warrant individual attention (DfEE 1999). What it does mean is that teachers need to allocate children to the most suitable group and provide work that is suitable for all members of that group. In terms of the UK National Curriculum, the teacher may have to choose the skills knowledge and understanding from earlier or later stages than is set down for the chldren's chronological age so that they can make progress and demonstrate what they can achieve. There is little point, for example, in trying to teach a child about multiplication if he or she does not yet have a well-developed understanding of addition.

While the overall provision for children with special educational needs is a whole-school or pre-school setting matter, it is the individual teachers responsibility to provide learning challenges for all pupils in his or her class, so that every child experiences success and achieves as high a standard as possible. This means closely matching the mathematics programme in the classroom to each child's needs. Adjusting not only the written work but also ensuring the teaching content allows pupils to develop knowledge and skills to suit their abilities.

 A Chance to Think

The National Numeracy Strategy points out that: many dyslexic learners make better progress if they work with practical versions of number tracks first, e.g. a 100-bead string. Estimated quantities may be counted into tens – structured tracks.

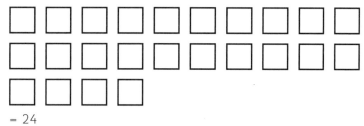

= 24

Quantities structured this way are easily 'rounded'.

Follow-up work on number lines should highlight number structures. For example, on a line to 100, the decades should be clearly demarcated. Pupils with learning difficulties also benefit from work on 'emptier' lines and 'emptier' materials, such as counting stacks. Such materials support the rounding of numbers (DfES, 2001)

This example comes from the National Numeracy Strategy daily mathematics lesson guidance to support pupils with dyslexia and dyscalculia. There are more examples of ways in which children with dyslexia and dyscalculia can be helped on the DfES website, at http://www.standards.dfes.gov.uk/numeracy/communities/inclusion.

All classes will have children who need special consideration and teachers will need to maintain high expectations so that children are able to take part in lessons fully and effectively and are given the opportunity to learn and enjoy mathematics. You should aim to include fully pupils with special educational needs in the daily mathematics lesson, if this is the class routine, or in any mathematical play opportunities that you have set up. All children will benefit from class oral and mental work, mathematical discussion and watching and listening as others explain their work.

The National Curriculum for England states that:

Teachers should take specific action to respond to pupils' diverse needs by:

A *creating effective learning environments*
B *securing their motivation and concentration*
C *providing equality of opportunity through teaching approaches*
D *using appropriate assessment approaches*
E *setting targets for learning* (DfEE, 1999)

Differentiation in the context of special educational needs should take account of extra support for less able children and suitable challenges for those whose attainment exceeds the expected level.

Planning for Children with Special Educational Needs

In considering how to deal with a wide range of needs, it is best if the work of different groups of children conforms to a common theme, so that all can feel part of the lesson or activity. Working on the same mathematical topic, but at different levels, allows for all to participate in class discussion. There are no easy ways to ensure effective differentiation. It requires excellent knowledge of the children's capabilities and attainment on a day-to-day basis. (Differentiation and class groupings are dealt with in more detail in Chapter 5.)

There are many problems associated with providing suitable and themed activities for a mixed-ability class, which become more difficult as the children become older. By the age of 11 there could be as much as a seven-year gap between the most and the least able (Cockcroft, 1982). Nevertheless, it is essential that teachers find successful methods of differentiation for the whole range of children in the class.

Matching the task correctly and appropriately to the level of the child's understanding is perhaps more crucial in mathematics than in any other subject. A poorly matched task can mean that the child does not understand at all. The result of this can be that he or she learns nothing (except that it may serve to underline the child's existing perception that mathematics is too difficult).

There are two main ways of differentiating for either low achievers or more able pupils. These are differentiation by task and differentiation by outcome (explained more fully in Chapter 5).

Sometimes tasks that can be differentiated by outcome can be difficult to find but most investigations lend themselves easily to this.

 A Chance to Think

The following task was differentiated by outcome. What resources would you provide for each of the children and what do you think you would expect to be the response of Anneka and Peter?

Anneka and Peter, aged 10, were each working by themselves on an investigation. Anneka was considered to be gifted mathematically, but Peter was a low achiever. They were given the following problem.

There are some chairs and a room full of children, some from Year 6 and some from the Reception class. The teacher decided that she wanted to put the chairs in a row for the children to sit on. She also said that the Reception class children were not allowed to sit side by side although the Year 6 children were. How many ways could you seat the children if there was only one chair? If there were two chairs, three chairs or four chairs, how many different ways could the children be seated then?

Anneka preferred to write down the sequences, using 6 for Year 6 and R for Reception. Peter used play people to represent the children and bricks to represent the chairs. (Children should always be given a choice when attempting this type of problem, as some will prefer to work more visually or practically than others.)

Peter found out that the ways that the children could be seated were:

1 chair – 2 ways
2 chairs – 3 ways
3 chairs – 5 ways
4 chairs – 8 ways

Anneke noticed that the number of seating arrangements possible was always a Fibonacci number:

No. of chairs				1	2	3	4	5	6	7	8	9	10	11	12	13	14
No. of ways				2	3	5	8	13	21	34	55	89	144	233	377	610	987
Fibonacci sequence	0	1	1	2	3	5	8	13	21	34	55	89	144	233	377	610	987

From this she was able to work out the number of arrangements for any number of chairs.

It is a good idea to create a bank of investigations and problems that are suitably challenging for the most able but at the same time capable of being accessed by the least able in the class; for some ideas see Haylock (1991).

Differentiation by task is perhaps the more common way of ensuring that children are working at a level that suits their knowledge and understanding. Problems can be used as the basis of differentiation by task, the advantage being that they link different strands of mathematics together and allow for interesting mathematical discussion around a theme.

A Chance to Think

For example, a class of 9-year-olds were arranging a party for their class of 30.

The children asked two parents to make the sandwiches at home. They decided that each child would have two small $1/4$-portion sandwiches. Each loaf has 22 slices including the crust. They needed to work out how many loaves each parent would need.

They decided to have crisps. There are 12 small packets of crisps in each large pack. Each child was to have one small packet of crisps. They had to work out how many large packs of crisps they needed.

They wanted squash to drink. Each bottle of squash contains 1 litre of juice. Each cup of drink requires 20 ml of squash. They worked out how many bottles of squash were needed for each child to have two cups.

They wanted to cut up Swiss rolls. Each Swiss roll can be cut into eight pieces. They worked out how many Swiss rolls were needed if each child was be allowed two pieces.

The tables needed covering. Children could sit eight to a table and each table was $1^{1}/_{2}$ m long. Paper table covering can be bought on a roll, each roll of which is 5 m long. They had to decide how many rolls were needed.

The paper plates came in packs of 12 and cups in packs of 50. They worked out how many packs of each they needed to buy.

Here is a price list. From this they worked out how much the party would cost.

Bread 37p a loaf; Butter 86p per pack; Fillings – ham £1.50/ten slices, cream cheese 95p a pack, eggs 98p for six; Crisps £1.22, Squash £1.50, Swiss rolls 54p; Table covering £1.50 per roll; Plates 98p per pack; Cups 98p per pack.

How would you match the parts of the problem to the children in the class to make sure that all had the opportunity to take part?

Sometimes in England schools purchase published mathematics schemes that have, so they claim, elements of differentiation within them. The trouble with these is that they are written remotely from the children in any particular class and therefore, although they may contain useful ideas and material, they should never be used piecemeal and should always be modified to meet the needs of your own particular group of children. Sometimes published schemes include plans that expect the lower-achieving children to complete a task on Tuesday that was considered too difficult on Monday. These plans should not be taken literally, as children will rarely have accumulated enough knowledge overnight to be able to tackle what was considered too difficult the day before.

Differentiated work must be worthwhile: this sounds obvious but it may be easier said than done. It is all too easy to give more able children extra practice in processes that they can already do and make the mathematics so simple for the least able that any challenge is lost. All children need to be involved in a whole-class discussion or activity. To facilitate this it is prudent to have a number of questions planned that are suitable for the lower achievers and some that are suitable for the higher achievers. Also, when drawing together the learning at the end of a lesson or day of activity remember to allow some of the less able children to report on their work, as all too often this is overlooked.

Some children may have gaps in their mathematical knowledge caused by missed or interrupted schooling or lack of mathematical experience at home. The teacher needs to identify any such gaps and be flexible enough to take account of them.

Teaching and Learning

It is the teacher's responsibility to create effective learning environments where all children can have access to the mathematics curriculum and all are encouraged to participate. Boys and girls, ethnic minorities and children with physical disabilities must be able to participate fully in the same curriculum. One way of ensuring this is to use a range of teaching styles that are appropriate to the learning styles of the children. Another is to vary the content of the lessons or mathematical activities and their presentation, for example by providing visual back-up to underpin verbal instructions. It is also a good idea to use a range of organizational approaches including individual and paired work, as well as ability and mixed-ability group work so that children can engage in mathematics with children who are experiencing similar difficulties and children who are enthusiastic mathematicians (see Chapter 5). Choice of materials that develop their understanding through the use of all the senses is another means of giving children access to learning. For some children this will be as simple as making sure that they have practical resources of a suitable size with which to work; for children with more complex needs it could mean the use of specialist aids or equipment, for example computer-based technology or specialist tools such as a hearing loop or Braille. For yet other children it will be necessary to provide some extra adult support, adapt tasks to make them more suitable for the child or even provide alternative activities.

 A Chance to Think

James, aged 8, had been diagnosed with dyspraxia. He was an intelligent boy who enjoyed mathematics and was particularly good at thinking mathematical processes through logically. His condition meant that his fine motor skills were underdeveloped. James was provided with a laptop and an adult was on hand to help so that he, like the other children in the class, could record his mathematical ideas for his teacher to see later.

As well as being able to access the content of the mathematics curriculum, children need opportunities to build up the relevant dispositions for becoming competent mathematicians, such as curiosity, logical thinking, interest, patience, confidence, challenge and perseverance. Children who have special educational needs are sometimes not given such opportunities.

Low achievers are sometimes given fairly mundane tasks, which are designed to help them to practise mathematical processes. Investigations and some of the more interesting mathematical problems are often given as 'add-on' tasks to be embarked on when the class activity is completed. Low achievers often complete work more slowly than other children in the class and so rarely have the time to tackle such interesting work, and even if they do, the moment of revelation, when the problem has been successfully solved, can be lost as someone else gets to the answer first. Children who find mathematics difficult often require continuous help and encouragement and need to be set short-term goals. The problem with this is that such pupils can be over-supported by adults in the classroom and as a consequence they do not develop the independence necessary to work things out for themselves. This can generate a feeling of inadequacy and disappointment, making them less willing to persevere next time. Children who are successful in mathematics are, by and large, those who often experience success, which maintains their confidence and interest.

On the other hand, children who are very competent are often insufficiently stretched. They do not have the chance to get 'stuck' on a problem, nor are they forced to work things through and develop solutions by conscious logical thinking. This means that their chances to develop patience and perseverance are reduced. It is by having to work through problems that their powers of reasoning and the ability to identify their own thought processes will improve. Many teachers are aware of this problem but often their desire to provide the most able mathematicians with suitable mathematical activities is overshadowed by the pressing need to cope with the demands of those who are mathematically least able (Wood, in Bearne, 1996: 42). Teachers need to achieve a balance here.

Different styles of learning and any particular difficulties need to be taken into account when assessing children with special educational needs and they should be given every chance and encouragement to demonstrate what they know and can do. On the basis of this, targets should be set for their learning that are built on their strengths, knowledge, interests and experience.

Dyscalculia

Dyscalculia is a condition that is peculiar to mathematics learning and affects a child's ability to acquire some mathematical skills. If a child is dyscalculic he or she may find it difficult 'to understand simple number concepts, lack an intuitive grasp of numbers, and have problems learning number facts and procedures' (DfES, 2001).

Children with dyscalculia can sometimes carry out mathematical procedures to produce a correct answer but they may not understand the process and usually because of this they will lack confidence. This condition is not well known or understood, owing to a paucity of research, and little is known about what causes it or how it should be treated.

In some children dyscalculia is the only problem and their difficulties will be confined to number and arithmetic. In these instances all other language and cognitive development will be in the normal range (DfES, 2001). In some children, however, dyscalculia is accompanied by difficulties with language and reading.

Reading and Language Difficulties

Sometimes children's mathematical skills are in advance of their language or reading skills but because their mathematical ability is not recognized, these children may be excluded from the work which they need to undertake. Providing appropriately challenging work for them is not an insurmountable problem but it does take thought.

Some children may have reading difficulties or may lack familiarity with English. This can slow their progress, not because they are unable to tackle the mathematics but because the reading is too difficult or the language – of the instructions or of the mathematical problem – is too complex. Showing the children the mathematical words on flash cards when explaining the use of mathematical language, so that the children can see what the words look like, or wall displays that show the uses of mathematical terms can sometimes help the children to cope with any reading that is necessary to the mathematics. It can be very supportive, at times, to enlist the help of an adult or more able child who can act as reader for the pupil with reading difficulties. Parents or other adults can be asked to help the child to recognize particular mathematical vocabulary in advance, in order to prepare for a mathematics lesson. Computer programs are usually enjoyable and motivating for the child and can be helpful in encouraging him or her to engage in extra practice.

Mathematical language is sometimes confusing for pupils as many of the words have a different meaning in everyday life, such as 'table' and 'difference'. As a result, children may have difficulty matching the mathematics to the task. The problem can be reduced by explaining the language fully and giving practical examples to show mathematical context in which the words are used.

All children benefit from explaining the mathematics that they are doing to other children or to the teacher or other adult. Some children, though, may have particular problems with oral work and may not have the vocabulary to explain what they mean. For such children, the chance to explicate by means of diagrams, drawings or practical apparatus may solve the problem. Alternatively some children may be able to cope with particular mathematical processes mentally but be unable to cope with the teacher's written methods for the same question that do not have the same written and mental algorithm, such as column addition and subtraction with larger numbers. In cases like this it can be beneficial to help the child to adapt his or her ideas into a useful working method.

 A Chance to Think

Marco in Year 7 was able to work out the addition 676 plus 257 in his head by adding the 100s then the 50 and lastly the 7. When he was asked to write this down as a column addition, however, he did this:

```
    676
+   257
_____

  81213
_____
```

He had not understood about carrying the tens into the next column on the left. His teacher decided to work with him to develop a strategy that he could understand. This is what they came up with:

```
                676
            +   257
            _____
add 200         876
add 50          926
add 7           933
            _____
```

Some children may have difficulty in listening to the teacher, because of a temporary or permanent hearing loss or because they have trouble in focusing their attention. In these circumstances it is good to sit the children near to the teacher or another adult so that discreet help and explanation can be given. Failing this, children can be put into pairs to work so that any missed instructions can be relayed from one child to another. Sometimes it may be even be necessary to help children with profound hearing loss to take part in mathematical activities by signing or other adult support.

For children with difficulty in hearing or understanding language, the use of visual clues is essential. Frequent use should be made of mathematical props and apparatus such as the number line, hundred square apparatus, interactive white board, computer programs and games and puzzles (see Chapter 4 on resources for more ideas).

Language can be a problem for a child with English as an additional language, particularly if his or her mathematical ability is underestimated simply because of the language barrier. It could be that they do not have the language to describe concepts that they actually understand. Children who are newly learning English should be expected to progress mathematically at the same rate as other children in the class and it should not be assumed that they have special educational needs in mathematics.

Teacher input to support the learner can be achieved by creating as many opportunities to model the spoken language as possible, speaking clearly and repeating instructions, simplifying the language and emphasizing the key mathematical words. It is also a good idea to put picture cues on individual or group-work written instructions. The mathematics should not be simplified unless the child with English as an additional language also has a special educational need in mathematics. It is often a good idea to ask the children to talk about the words used for mathematical signs and symbols in their own language while emphasizing the names of these in English. This helps the children to make connections between what is already familiar to them and the terms used in English.

Children with English as an additional language, along with the rest of the class should be encouraged to join in the singing of number rhymes or take part in chanting the counting numbers or multiplication tables, activities that help all children to develop their number sense.

They should also be given the opportunity to listen carefully and respond where they can. The teacher should not expect the children to present their response orally in the early stages of learning English but should allow them to watch and listen to the fluent English speakers in the class explaining their methods on a board or flip chart. Later the teacher can invite the child with English as an additional language to demonstrate his or her work either on a flip chart or by using apparatus, without pressure to provide an oral explanation. If the child has been working in a pair or small group then other members of the group can provide the oral explanation.

Achmed and Fatima both had little English and although they could understand numbers when they were written down they both found trying to translate from the spoken word difficult. In order to help the children to develop the necessary English vocabulary their teacher always held up written numbers and symbol flashcards when asking the children to work out calculations mentally. All the children had small white boards and board markers so that they could write down and then hold up the answers for the teacher to see. As there was no need for the children to speak the answer, Achmed and Fatima were able to participate in the same way as the other children and so did not feel left out or isolated.

Working in pairs or suitable groups also becomes important because other children can provide support for the English learner. Talk within a peer group when working on a common problem, doing practical work or playing mathematical games can help all the children to make sense of and apply ideas, not least the child for whom English is an additional language. Group work also allows the teacher the opportunity to give focused input to and make assessments of a small number of children. This might be particularly beneficial to children who, because of language difficulties, have not been able to follow the main lesson input. It will show the teacher what they can do – they may even be better than their peers.

Many children respond well to the use of ICT as a teaching and learning tool. Computer programs, video and or audio materials are especially good at supporting the mathematical learning of children with language and communication difficulties. Throughout mathematics teaching and assessment, written materials need to be readily understood, non-mathematical language needs to be kept simple and to the minimum and materials can also be presented in alternative formats such as using larger print or extra use of picture cues and symbols.

Pupils with Sensory or Physical Disabilities

Children with physical or sensory disabilities do not need to work on a mathematics programme separate from the rest of the pupils in the class and will, in fact, benefit from working alongside their peers. Not all children with physical or sensory disabilities will have need of extra provision but where they do the potential problems are likely to be access and the need for extra support, rather than difficulties with the mathematical content. Of course they should be provided with mathematical materials and equipment to meet their particular needs, for example technological aids, tactile materials and adapted measuring equipment.

 A Chance to Think

It is easy inadvertently to isolate a pupil in the classroom and thought should be given to the best way to make every child feel part of the class. Claire, a special educational needs coordinator, was watching a class of 7-year-old pupils engaged in a numeracy lesson. She noticed that Abigail, who was in a wheelchair and had fine motor skill problems, was at times isolated from the rest of the children. In the first part of the lesson the class was seated on the carpet. Abigail could not sit on the floor, so her wheelchair was placed behind the group. She therefore sat above the other children. Claire suggested later to the class teacher that perhaps some of the other children could have sat on chairs behind the group so that Abigail was not alone at the back.

Later in the lesson, because she needed to use a keyboard with the support of a classroom assistant, Abigail was sent to the side of the classroom to work on the class computer. Although the work she was given was similar to that given to other pupils of similar ability, she was again physically isolated, and this time she also had her back to her peers. Claire suggested that perhaps Abigail could use the teacher's laptop and sit at a table with the rest of her peers. The class teacher, having made sure that Abigail had the same curriculum access as the others, had not realized that Abigail was being physically isolated.

Sometimes children with physical or sensory problems take longer to settle at or to complete tasks. This means that they should be given extra time to do written work or to manipulate practical apparatus.

Building Self-esteem and Enthusiasm

Many people find mathematics difficult and it is very easy to undermine children's confidence in their mathematical ability. In order to raise their confidence, all children need to feel secure and able to contribute fully. The teacher needs to create a supportive learning environment which allows time for pupils to engage in learning. All of the children in a class, including those with special educational needs, should be encouraged to express their ideas to each other in small groups and to the rest of the class. When children are able to demonstrate their mathematical understandings and ideas, either in written form or with apparatus, this helps not only to clarify their own method of working but also to allow the other children in the class to develop their understanding. Sometimes a pupil who has just mastered a mathematical skill or process can explain it in an alternative way and in terms that the other children can understand.

Children's interest and motivation can be enhanced by taking account of, and catering for, their interests and cultural background, using a variety of activities set in different contexts and materials that reflect social and cultural diversity and provide positive images of race, gender and disability (DfEE, 1999).

 A Chance to Think

Maisie and Jack had visited the local harbour with their class. The teacher set a variety of mathematical tasks for the children there from which they were allowed to choose. Jack chose to count the number of fishing boats that were moored in the harbour and work out how many more could tie up before the mooring area reached its capacity. Maisie was interested in the lifeboat and, as they had been told the speed at which it usually travelled, she wanted to work out how long it would take to reach a fishing boat that was in trouble four miles out from the shore.

Children will inevitably place a variety of interpretations on their work and produce a variety of outcomes. If they are to feel confident and enthusiastic about mathematics, these alternative responses should be welcomed and their opinions and efforts respected and valued. Mathematical targets should also be set that are attainable and yet challenging, as small successes will help to develop their self-esteem and confidence in their ability to learn mathematics. Feedback should be honest but positive and an effort should be made to reflect the importance of mathematical working and the child's developing dispositions, rather than purely on whether the answer is right.

As we have seen in Chapter 5, it can be productive to explore different ways of grouping the children so that the more able have the opportunity to explain their understanding to the lower achievers and those that are experiencing difficulties get the opportunity to engage in mathematical discussion.

Using Other Adults

It is of course the teacher who has primary responsibility for the welfare and progress of children with special educational needs and who has the expertise to deal with any problems that arise. That said, it is also beneficial at times for the children to have the extra help and support of a teaching assistant or other competent adult who will ensure that the children interpret instructions correctly, sum up and remind them of teaching points and check that the children have all the equipment that they need for the task, all in the interests of consolidating the children's learning.

If classroom or teaching assistants are to be used specifically to support and enhance the learning of SEN children, however, they should not be expected to do this without good training and clear guidance. Adult helpers in the classroom may even lack confidence in mathematics themselves and need to enhance their own mathematical knowledge and understanding before they can help the children. Teaching assistants and other adult helpers may particularly need support in developing their questioning skills, because appropriate questioning encourages children's participation and enthusiasm. It may be necessary for the teacher to provide the helping adult with a series of questions and prompts for the children.

Ideally the learning support assistant should be involved in the planning as this gives the helper an insight into the teacher's expectations about what the children are to learn. It is also an opportunity for the class teacher to discuss with the teaching assistant any specialist equipment that will be needed or any individualized programme that has been devised and put into place for a child. Although the ideal is not always attainable, teachers should always make sure that the teaching assistants know exactly what their role is and what the children are expected to achieve.

Assessment of children with special educational needs should to be ongoing so that even small successes are picked up. The teaching assistant or other adult can be invaluable in collecting such evidence as well as noticing any difficulties, misconceptions or mistakes.

Summary

In this chapter we have looked at the need for teachers to consider all children in their planning to enable all to take part in and enjoy mathematics lessons fully.

Some children may find it difficult to access the normal class mathematics curriculum because of cultural, physical, sensory, behavioural, emotional or neurological differences, or because of a legacy of poor learning that affects current progress or because they are ahead of their expected chronological age group. Matching the mathematics teaching appropriately to the level of the child's understanding is crucial in mathematics; one way of doing this is by the differentiation of work, either by task or by outcome.

Teachers need to make sure that the children have the opportunity to develop their understanding through the use of all of their available senses and experiences, which means that materials have to be provided that allow the children to access the learning.

Finally, it should be remembered that children with special educational needs are not essentially different from other children and it is more beneficial to the teaching and learning of mathematics if the teacher is able to emphasize the links between what the children know and what they are to learn rather than emphasizing what is not understood.

Reflective Questions

- Can you identify some groups of children who might need special consideration in the mathematics classroom?
- How might you create effective mathematical learning environments for all children?
- What strategies could you use to secure the motivation and enthusiasm of all children?
- What is the role of other adults in ensuring the best possible experience for the children with special educational needs?

REFERENCES AND FURTHER READING

Cockcroft, W. (1982) *Mathematics Counts: Report of the Commission of Enquiry into the Teaching of Mathematics in Schools*, London: HMSO.

DfEE (1999) *The National Curriculum*.

DfEE (1999) *The National Numeracy Strategy*.

DfES (2001) *Special Educational Needs Code of Practice*, Nottinghamshire: DfES publications.

DfES website (2001) 'Guidance to support pupils with dyslexia and dyscalculia', 'Guidance to support pupils with hearing impairment', 'Guidance to support pupils with speech and language difficulties', 'Guidance to support pupils with visual impairments' http://www.standards.dfes.gov.uk/numeracy/communities/inclusion.

Haylock, D. (1991) *Teaching Mathematics to Low Attainers 8–12*, London: Paul Chapman.

Wood, A. (1996) 'Differentiation in primary mathematics', in Bearne, E. (ed.) *Differentiation and Diversity*, London: Routledge.

www.standards.dfes.gov.uk/numeracy/prof_dev/features/maths.

Coordinating Mathematics

INTRODUCTION

The previous chapters have largely been concerned with the role of the individual class teacher or practitioner. This chapter aims to put this role more firmly within the whole-school context.

The design of primary education generally draws upon the model of children working with one teacher throughout a year, covering each area of the curriculum within the same class. There may be some movement between classes where schools use a system of setting for core subjects, but a belief in a secure relationship with one teacher usually characterizes the organization of a primary school. Pre-school settings and reception classes will often have a number of adults with whom the children work. These adults will usually either plan cooperatively or be under the direction of a reception class teacher or nursery manager, and they will almost certainly be expected to teach across the curriculum in the same way as a primary school teacher. In a secondary school, by contrast, more specialist teaching is provided by expert teachers in each subject, and the children move from teacher to teacher during the school day.

Consequently, the role of the primary teacher or pre-school practitioner to inspire, support and challenge learning in children across the curriculum can be intimidating. The teacher or practitioner is expected to have a good subject knowledge in a number of curricular areas, alongside an understanding of appropriate teaching and learning styles for that subject, progression and continuity, common misconceptions, and a critical awareness of resources including ICT. Clearly, even after a lengthy period of training, all teachers need to view their teacher education as simply the beginning of a career of continuing professional development.

It is usual in primary schools, which includes reception classes, for one member of staff to take responsibility for each area of the curriculum. This teacher may be called the curriculum coordinator or subject leader. This system aims to support classroom teachers in their task of providing effective teaching in all areas of the curriculum, linking the pre-school, primary and secondary systems of organizing education. The head teacher takes overall responsibility for the curriculum, but is supported in this role by the curriculum coordinator who often has much more in-depth and current knowledge of the teaching and learning within the subject.

This chapter therefore explores:

- The need for one member of staff to have a coordinating role
- The role of the mathematics coordinator
- When a class teacher might call upon the support of a curriculum coordinator
- How a class teacher might obtain an overview of teaching mathematics across the school
- The use of a whole-school audit to develop mathematics teaching throughout the school

This chapter will provide the new and training teacher with a general, if not full understanding of the role of the mathematics coordinator, which should enable him or her to work effectively with curriculum coordinators and to understand the importance of whole-school audits and staff development.

The Need for One Member of Staff to Have a Coordinating Role

It is at the very least desirable, perhaps even necessary for one member of staff to have an overview of the teaching of mathematics across the school or pre-school setting. This overview will ensure continuity and progression in learning across the school or setting, support and inform decisions about what mathematics will be taught and how, oversee the appropriate allocation of resources and avoid the purposeless repetition of activities.

Continuity and progression throughout the school are important for laying the foundations for the mathematics that comes later and judging whether planning for each age group is appropriate.

 A Chance to Think

For example, the children in Year 6 at Swain Community Primary School were to be taught the decomposition method of written subtraction. It was important for the coordinator to make sure that throughout Key Stages 1 and 2 the children were prepared for this by experiencing the partitioning of numbers in a variety of flexible ways.

Scrutiny of teachers' termly planning at Highbridge Primary School allowed the mathematics coordinator to identify that in Year 1 too much was being expected of children, but in Year 4 too little was expected. The coordinator, in discussion with the teachers, created revised termly plans, thereby ensuring smooth progression throughout the school.

Coordinators can also support and contribute to decisions about the provision for individual children with special mathematics-related needs, and share this information between staff effectively.

 A Chance to Think

Consider the case of Billy, an able child in Year 2. It was decided that his mathematical learning should be accelerated so that he had access to the content of the curriculum for Year 3. The mathematics coordinator ensured that Billy's next teacher in Year 3 was fully informed of the curriculum covered and appropriate teaching and learning styles for the following year. The coordinator also made sure that as Billy entered Year 6, she supported the class teacher in providing appropriate experiences that related to the curriculum for Year 7. The coordinator also liaised with the child's secondary school. As can be seen, the decision made in Year 2 to accelerate the child into the Year 3 curriculum had far-reaching consequences.

The coordinator will usually oversee the allocation of resources to ensure that children in the early years of education have the opportunity to develop the skills that they will need later. This may be facilitated, for instance, by making sure that resources such as telephones and money tills are on hand for the play house area or that number tracks, which aid counting and relate well to children's experiences of board games, are available. Naturally the resources will become more specialized to suit the age and stage of the children as they progress, for example number tracks will be superseded by number lines thus giving a more accurate model of the number system. Similarly, the coordinator will ensure that the balance scales used with younger children are replaced by dial scales the children become more advanced. (See Chapter 4 for more detail about the suitability of resources.)

The coordinator should try to eliminate the purposeless repetition of activities by monitoring the termly and perhaps weekly plans so as to be able to track the experiences of specific classes or groups of children. Termly planning may indicate a clear and smooth progression from one year to the next, but weekly planning may identify unnecessary repetition of investigation activities, practical work or mathematical situations. Purposeful repetition of activities can, however, be beneficial but only if the activity has been covered previously and the practitioner is aware of the learning that took place so that progression is ensured. It can be useful, for example, to return to a combination activity that asks the children to explore the number of possibilities when dressing a teddy with three different hats, three different T-shirts and three different pairs of shorts. Repetition of the activity can help the children meet the objective of listing the possibilities methodically to establish that all are counted once. It can also generate further examples of possibilities with different numbers of hats, T-shirts and pairs of shorts, therefore providing valuable opportunities for the children to reach general statements and to explain their reasoning.

To keep all members of staff informed of the mathematical activities that the children have already encountered, the coordinator should see either that formal written records are passed between teachers or, if he or she identifies repetition in planning, that meetings are set up for informal exchange of information.

The mathematics curriculum coordinator therefore takes a whole-school or whole-setting role in developing teaching and learning. In the first years of their teaching career, class teachers and other practitioners are usually and rightly concerned primarily with the children in their own class or group, with relationships within that, with maintaining secure and positive working environments and with ensuring the planning and assessing of appropriate learning. However, as their experience grows, teachers become much more aware of the way their teaching is influenced by the teaching and learning that has taken place the year before and how their work with the children this year will impact on their learning next year. There follows a natural progression in the development of the teacher's focus from classroom or group to whole school or setting. Becoming a curriculum coordinator in a school therefore is often the next step in a teacher's professional development, after a number of years as classroom teacher.

What is the Role of the Mathematics Coordinator within a School Setting?

According to the DfES *(Teachers' Standards Framework: Helping You Develop, 2001)*,

Subject leaders provide professional leadership and management for a subject to secure high quality teaching, effective use of resources and improved standards of learning and achievement for all pupils.

The role of the mathematics coordinator is to enhance and support the teaching and learning of mathematics in every classroom in the school. The responsibility does not lie solely with the mathematics coordinator, but is shared with the head teacher, senior management and to some extent every member of staff in the school. The mathematics coordinator has the advantage of being a classroom teacher who can try ideas out in the classroom and critically evaluate and share them, support colleagues with a sympathetic ear, as he or she faces similar challenges, and lead by example. It may be more difficult for a head teacher, who has little opportunity for teaching, to promote and sustain change. The co-ordinator's role can be eased by promoting a professional dialogue between members of staff that is equal and open.

The role of the coordinator of mathematics may involve:

- Acting as an example of a good teacher of mathematics
- Keeping up to date with current issues and developments in mathematics education
- Providing support for the subject knowledge of other teachers
- Ensuring progression and continuity in the teaching and learning of mathematics across the school
- Monitoring teaching and learning of mathematics across the school
- Providing staff development to introduce, promote and sustain changes in order to enhance teaching and learning
- Managing the mathematics budget and organizing resources
- Monitoring whole-school standards in mathematics and setting targets
- Providing support in the form of written policies and guidelines

Acting as an Example

The coordinator, first and foremost, will endeavour to act as an example of a good teacher of mathematics. There should be no expectation that the coordinator's lessons are always exemplary. In fact, it is often the coordinator who tries out and evaluates new ideas, resources and teaching styles, some of which succeed better than others. However, the coordinator must have developed clear and justifiable principles and beliefs for his or her own teaching of mathematics and may be asked to provide demonstration lessons or to observe or work with other teachers in their classrooms. Therefore, the coordinator should be able to identify and promote features of teaching and learning that are of a high standard. This involves a great deal of reflection on what is effective teaching and learning in mathematics, allowing the coordinator to introduce and support changes when these are necessary.

Keeping up to Date

The coordinator's reflection on teaching and learning in mathematics should be informed by the reading of research summaries in the media and journals, and maintaining a critical awareness of changes and initiatives in mathematics education. Time is short for most teachers' reading, and therefore the staff can work as a team, providing up-to-date information for each other in specific areas of the curriculum.

Support for Subject Knowledge

There are high expectations for teachers' subject knowledge across the curriculum, and the subject coordinator has a part to play in supporting teachers in specific subject knowledge issues. It may be that teachers have particularly able children who ask searching questions or who require more advanced mathematical resources. In fact, any child may ask a difficult question, such as 'Why do even numbers multiplied by odd numbers always give even numbers?' This is particularly true in a school that promotes discussion of methods and investigational ways of working. The mathematics coordinator may not always have the answers to such questions at his or her fingertips, but should have access to online information and books and journals that will provide answers.

Ensuring Progression and Continuity

Some coordinators may provide termly or even weekly planning for teachers in order to ensure progression and continuity. Judgement needs to be exercised here, as while tightly planned work does provide clear guidelines it can restrict teachers' ability to adapt to individual learning needs and to make cross-curricular connections. Looser guidelines have the same benefit in terms of progression but allow teachers creativity and flexibility.

Monitoring Teaching and Learning

Coordinators can monitor teaching and learning across the school by scrutinizing the planning of teachers but they may also use various other strategies, as teachers often have to adapt plans quite radically to meet the needs of the children in their classes. For example, they may be released from their classroom to observe colleagues or to work alongside them. Equally, other teachers may come to observe the coordinator teach mathematics, which then promotes a feedback discussion. The coordinator may assess work by asking to look at samples of children's written mathematics and ask teachers across the school to undertake a similar investigation with their classes, which allows the coordinator to collect and monitor the work of children across the school in the same area of mathematics. Children's work can be celebrated by mounting a display of examples. Later on in this chapter we will consider other strategies that coordinators may use to familiarize themselves with the actual provision in the school.

Providing Staff Development

As a result of monitoring the current provision or of the implementation of initiatives from outside the school, the coordinator will often be in the position of introducing and supporting change. This may take the form of leading staff meetings; providing input on changes to the curriculum or new teaching styles; or discussing examples, say, of new recording systems; or trying out new resources and providing a critical evaluation of them. The coordinator may support staff individually, for example in the use of ICT, or organize training courses for staff and feed back from their own training. This aspect of the coordinator's role can be the most challenging and difficult.

Budget and Resources

Management of the mathematics budget and resources is another responsibility that falls to the coordinator, consisting of auditing current resources, surveying the staff's requirements and ordering and organizing resources. Published schemes can be particularly expensive and their purchase needs to be considered in depth.

Monitoring Whole-school Standards and Setting Targets

This aspect of the coordinator's role may involve analysing children's performance in a range of statutory and purchased tests, alongside teacher assessments. Targets may be set in terms of children's future performance in tests or in terms of particular areas of interest for the school such as creativity. The coordinator is often required to develop a subject-specific development plan to link with the subject-specific budget for mathematics. This will demonstrate how the coordinator anticipates the development of mathematics over the coming years. Often this is used to inform governors of progress within the subject area.

Written Policies and Guidelines

The coordinator may provide a written policy for mathematics, alongside guidelines that relate to mathematics within other more general policies such as those on marking and assessment, inclusion, assessment and record keeping, transition between Key Stages, cross-curricular learning, homework and involving parents in their children's learning. Policies and guidelines should reflect the common beliefs of the staff as a whole in respect of the features of effective teaching and learning of mathematics.

Although these guidelines refer specifically to schools there is no reason why pre-school settings should not use this model to enhance their own mathematics curriculum. Having one member of staff responsible for the mathematical development of the children is a good way of ensuring that mathematics education pervades the whole of the children's experience in pre-school and does not become an add-on activity that takes place only in a constrained and rather formal way.

In England, inspectors or LEA advisers visiting the school often look for evidence that policies reflect consistent practice; nursery inspectors expect to see effective planning, suitable resources and the use of the pre-school setting for mathematics.

How Should a Class Teacher Use the Support of a Curriculum Coordinator?

Classroom teachers and pre-school practitioners can feel an immense pressure to be expert in every curriculum area, certainly in the earlier years of their teaching career. It is now recognized that initial teacher education and training for pre-school are only the beginning of a career-long period of continuing professional development. Knowing when and how to call on the support of colleagues is an important skill of a teacher or practitioner, leading to increased teamwork in the staff and personal professional development.

A teacher or practitioner may call on the mathematics coordinator for help in the following ways:

- When planning the first term's work for a new class or group, particularly in a new school or setting
- When meeting the learning needs of individual children
- To clarify subject knowledge issues
- To ensure appropriate use of resources
- To establish how ICT can be used to enhance teaching and learning of mathematics

Planning for the First Term

A newly appointed practitioner, teacher or student teacher will need to have details of the proposed termly planning for his or her new class or group and the curriculum covered in the previous year. A meeting with the coordinator early on in the term or at the end of the previous term, before the teacher or practitioner takes up the appointment, can help to establish the expectations for the coming year and to give some idea of whether the class or group in question are working at an appropriate level for their age. The coordinator may also help to set up a meeting with the previous class teacher to transfer more detailed records. There may be systems of collaborative planning in year groups or across the setting, of which the newly appointed teachers or practitioners will need to be made aware. The coordinator can also give a new member of staff an idea of the degree of flexibility exercised by the school or setting. For example termly planning in school can often be split into short topics which are repeated during the year.

The sample medium-term plans and unit plans produced by the English National Numeracy Strategy are modelled in this way, with perhaps five days dedicated to the teaching of place value towards the beginning of each half term. For examples see www.standards.dfes.gov.uk/numeracy/publications. This may be appropriate in many cases, but some practitioners may prefer to use the plans flexibly, spending more or less time on each topic than suggested in the strategy in accordance with the particular learning needs of the children in their classes. Other teachers prefer to link their teaching of mathematics to cross-curricular themes or to trips and visits.

The coordinator can guide the newly appointed members of staff on the conventions in the school for planning creatively. At the planning stage, the coordinator will be able to inform teachers or practitioners on, for example, the policy of the school towards mental and written calculation strategies. There should be clear expectations about the strategies that are taught in each year group and how these fit into the progression throughout the school.

For example, if in Year 6 the school has decided not to teach long division, but to use the method of repeated subtraction as the written algorithm for division, this will have implications for all year groups in the school. Repeated subtraction can be used in a very simple form throughout Key Stages 1 and 2 in preparation for Year 6. The coordinator will be able to give advice and support in this area.

Meeting Individual Learning Needs

When class teachers or practitioners become familiar with their new class or group, they may identify learning needs that are new or unfamiliar. The coordinator, alongside the Special Educational Needs Coordinator (SENCO), in schools, or member of staff responsible for special educational needs, in a pre-school setting, can offer valuable support to the teacher in meeting these needs. For example, there may be a particularly able child in the class. The coordinator will oversee the transfer of records on this child, and inform a newly appointed teacher or practitioner of the policy of the school towards this particular child, be it policy of enrichment or acceleration. In either case, the class teacher may need access to appropriate teaching and learning resources. Strategies to ensure that the child has opportunities to discuss his or her mathematical learning can also be shared. One able child in a class can become isolated.

In other cases the coordinators can provide support in meeting the needs of children who find mathematics difficult, again with the help of the SENCO or member of staff responsible for special educational needs. When a child's learning causes concern in mathematics, the coordinator can provide informal support in the form of discussion. Often talking through a child's needs with an experienced teacher or practitioner can identify patterns of behaviour and suggest strategies to minimize barriers to learning. The coordinator can be called upon to look at samples of practical or written work or even to observe the child at work in the classroom. Again, another teacher's or practitioner's viewpoint can throw light on what at first seems to be a very difficult situation. The coordinator may work alongside the class teacher or practitioner, trying out strategies to support learning or releasing the class teacher or practitioner to do so. The coordinator may help to identify specific learning difficulties or be able to refer children to agencies who can do this.

Mathematics coordinators should have access to information on supporting the learning of children with specific learning difficulties such as dyscalculia, visual impairment or autistic spectrum disorders. Information of this kind can be found on www.standards.dfes.gov.uk/numeracy/publications. This information may inform targets set for the child and the timetabling of teaching or nursery assistants.

The mathematics coordinator will not have any magic formula to meet the mathematical needs of every child in the school or setting. By working together as a team, however, staff can feel supported in meeting needs of all of the children, which otherwise could leave them feeling isolated and disheartened.

Clarifying Subject Knowledge

When a teacher or practitioner is unsure of an appropriate way of explaining, modelling or demonstrating an idea or mathematical term or of using a resource, it is appropriate to ask for support from the mathematics coordinator. This should not be seen as a sign of weakness by staff members.

For example, a teacher can teach a class that to multiply a number by ten, the rule is to add a zero. This gives the children a quick and easy method of remembering how to multiply by ten, but is not based on understanding. When children multiply decimal fractions by ten, the rule will not help them. Errors such as the following may occur:

$5.8 \times 10 = 5.80$

or

$5.8 \times 10 = 50.8$

Other errors can occur when teachers do not have a fully developed understanding of mathematical vocabulary. Children need to have a full understanding of terms such as subtraction in order to develop concepts fully and to recognize subtraction in its many forms when solving problems. Teachers' use of examples to define vocabulary can also limit children's understanding. For example, a teacher who introduces the idea of parallel lines showing examples of pairs of lines that are all either horizontal or vertical, have nothing drawn in between them and are always the same length is establishing a limited definition of concept of parallel. The children may not recognize the following as parallel lines:

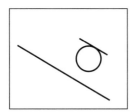

The coordinator can also support teachers and practitioners in their own interest in mathematics and has a role to play in supporting teachers' and practitioners' responses to children's probing questions, and in promoting the fascination for mathematics in both teachers and children, which is essential for creative and effective teaching and learning.

For example, a teacher may be teaching simple investigations such as:

Add together three consecutive numbers. What do you notice?
Add together five consecutive numbers. What do you notice?
Predict what you will find when you add together seven and nine consecutive numbers.

By generating a number of examples, the children may establish that when adding three consecutive numbers, the total is three times the middle number. When adding five consecutive numbers the total is five times the middle number. The children or the teacher may wonder why this happens. The coordinator may be able to explain this to the teacher or provide resources that do so, by using pictures or algebraic symbols:

This picture shows 3 + 4 + 5
If we rearrange the picture, then we can show that 3 + 4 + 5 = 4 + 4 + 4

Or to show this in a more general way, if we call the middle number n, then:

$$(n–1) + n + (n + 1) = n + n + n$$

Appropriate use of resources, including ICT

A new member of staff or a teacher changing classes or age group may call on the coordinator to help identify the resources he or she will need.

The coordinator will be able to offer advice such as:

- Which resources are appropriate given the plans in place
- Which resources should be found in the classroom
- How resources can minimize barriers to learning and assessment
- Where shared resources can be found across the school
- How to order resources if these are necessary
- How to use resources that are unfamiliar to the teacher
- How to organize resources in the classroom to ensure the children use them independently and are able to make decisions about which resources are appropriate for the task in hand
- How to organize time and space for play in the classroom and how to use these for assessment and teaching of mathematics
- Appropriate resources for outside play
- Appropriate published resources in the school and on the Internet and how these can be best used

ICT tends to be thought of separately to other resources as it is a growing area with the assumed potential to enhance the teaching and learning of mathematics. The mathematics coordinator and ICT coordinator should be able to work together to advise teachers and practitioners about the best use of ICT.

At the beginning of the term, a class teacher or practitioner who perhaps lacks confidence in using ICT may find it useful to meet with the mathematics coordinator and discuss and annotate the termly plan with possible links to ICT that is available in the school or setting. For example, shape and space topics could be linked to the Roamer or the use of Logo. The coordinator may be able to identify interactive websites for use with children in particular topics or websites that offer teachers advice and ideas. Specific software purchased by the school or setting may link to other topics on the plan. The coordinator will be able to offer advice as to how and when calculators and interactive whiteboards can be best used with the class.

Where the school has an ICT suite, the incorporation of ICT into mathematics lessons will be timetabled towards the beginning of the year. The coordinator may advise scheduling blocks of time, say a week of sessions for mathematics each term or one session a week or fortnight throughout the year. Portable laptops may have similar timetables. Where computers are kept in the classroom, the coordinator may be able to help to organize the sharing of computers to allow larger groups of children to use them for blocks of time, or the sharing of data projectors and interactive whiteboards.

The better a new teacher understands the role of the mathematics coordinator the more effectively he or she will work as part of the staff team and be able to draw appropriately on the support of others. This should not be seen as a sign of weakness but as part of continuing professional development.

Developing the Role of the Mathematics Coordinator

Teachers generally become mathematics coordinators by developing their position in the school or by transferring to another school to take on the-role. Mathematics coordinators as such do not exist in pre-school settings but some of the ideas we give here are applicable to such settings.

As we have seen, the coordinator or subject leader takes a whole-school view of mathematics, rather than focusing entirely on the needs of his or her own class of children. This view usually takes a few years of teaching to develop.

A teacher who wants to become a coordinator should seek professional advice from the head teacher, who may be able to recommend continuing professional development courses. There are also various books and publications that discuss in more detail how a career may develop in this direction. They are given at the end of this chapter.

One method of gaining an insight into what it is to have such a whole-school responsibility is to shadow the current coordinator. With the head teacher's permission it may be possible to undertake an audit of mathematics teaching and learning in order to become familiar with the current provision for mathematics across the school. This is an excellent strategy which allows the coordinator to prepare a development plan aimed at raising standards but based on the realities of current provision.

An audit might involve the following:

You might begin by reading the latest inspection report on the school, looking in particular at the comments on mathematics. This will provide a snapshot of practice in the school at one particular time, and can be a useful insight into current provision, although it should be used critically. Other general reports on the inspections of mathematics throughout the country and evaluations of initiatives such as the National Numeracy Strategy can give some guidelines and principles to aid the coordinator's judgements and to provide a wider view. These can be found on websites such as:

www.standards.dfes.gov.uk/numeracy

www.ofsted.gov.uk

www.qca.org.uk

Documents which detail the performance of the school in statutory testing and provide a comparison with national levels and with similar schools. Again, these can give a feel for the level of standards in the school. There may be additional data on children's performance in non-statutory testing, which can be analysed with reference to the data on the QCA website: www.qca.org.uk

Testing can give a fairly accurate picture of the learning of children but only at one particular time in a particular set of circumstances. The coordinator will also want to assess a wider picture by considering the children's creativity, their ability to think for themselves, their enjoyment of mathematics, their confidence, their ability to work with others, their speaking and listening skills in mathematics and their application and transfer of mathematical skills and knowledge. These aspects of children's learning cannot be fully assessed by formal testing.

Scrutiny of teachers' current termly planning can give an overview of the mathematics curriculum covered in each year group. A check against the National Curriculum and/or the National Numeracy Strategy will allow the potential coordinator to make a rudimentary judgement about the coverage of key concepts and vocabulary.

In order to judge continuity and progression in the curriculum covered in the school, a teacher can take one area of mathematics, such as place value, and draw up a simple model of expected progression, based on his or her own knowledge and experience of teaching. This would list some of the main concepts in a logical order that should result in a firm understanding of place value – of course with the proviso that mathematical learning is not always linear.

In England, for example, the teacher can refer to the National Numeracy Strategy and National Curriculum to modify this progression map, noting how the school's planning compares in this area of mathematics. It is often easier to judge planning by taking one specific area of mathematics in this way.

A scrutiny of current weekly plans, if any, will add further information on how termly plans are actually put into practice in the classroom. Weekly plans can give details of:

- How objectives are translated into teaching and learning activities
- How vocabulary is introduced and consolidated
- How teachers differentiate work
- How teaching assistants are employed
- How the plenary is used to reinforce and assess learning
- How problem-solving and investigational work are tackled
- Whether teachers avoid contributing to possible common misconceptions
- The balance between activities that are visual, oral and kinaesthetic
- How children are grouped for activities

Weekly plans will also reveal teachers' beliefs about teaching and learning mathematics. For example, the weekly plans of a teacher who believes in the importance of cross-curricular learning and of making connections within mathematics itself will look very different from those of a teacher who is focused on the coverage of certain mathematical content.

An audit can list and evaluate the mathematical resources in the school. These are probably kept both in individual classrooms and in a central location. Simply listing what the school has in terms of resources can provide a coordinator or potential coordinator with a starting position for allocating budgets and buying new resources. In a small school, it may be a better use of money to buy a smaller number of the more expensive resources, such as scales and capacity containers, and keep them centrally. Everyday resources such as number squares, place value cards and calculators will need to be purchased in greater numbers to be kept in classrooms. Resources that are kept in classrooms where they are not used can be redistributed, and any that are out of date or broken should naturally be discarded. If mathematics is to be valued by teachers and children, then resources must be of a good quality.

Of course, the way in which resources are used is as important as the resources themselves. Teachers may use inappropriate resources, or use them in inappropriate ways, perhaps because of insecure subject knowledge or a misunderstanding.

Similar scrutiny of published resources is also revealing of teachers' attitudes and practices. Where published schemes of work are used rigidly, it may be because teachers are short of time or lack the confidence and knowledge to generate their own ideas, which might be linked more carefully to individual children's needs. Many teachers use schemes that they openly criticize, and this critical evaluation should be encouraged. Published schemes can be extremely useful when they are used critically and not followed blindly. An audit of published resources throughout the school may identify old and out-of-date books, which can be discarded, and more valuable resources that are not being used by the most appropriate year groups.

Look also at ICT resources. Unless ICT is used extensively to enhance teaching and learning of mathematics, the coordinator may find few resources specifically aimed at mathematics or resources that are not used effectively. For example, teachers may use mathematics games only for early finishers or as rewards in a free choice session. Learning may well take place, but this is not planned and is left to chance. Again, undertaking a scrutiny of ICT resources and linking them to termly and weekly plans will show whether ICT is being used purposefully. A short one-to-one support session with the coordinator can help a teacher gain confidence in using relevant software. Or the purchase of particular software and hardware can be negotiated with the ICT coordinator, who may have a larger budget to spend.

As already noted, scrutiny of a sample of children's written work across the school can help the coordinator to gain a feel for the level of work for each year group, to look for progression and continuity and to see whether there are shared and common expectations. For example, the coordinator can look for:

- Children recording mathematics in ways that are meaningful for them, and refining these towards standard ways of recording
- Children solving routine and non-routine problems
- Cross-curricular links
- The effective use of games, visits and stories to stimulate mathematical curiosity
- A variety of activities that appeal to varying learning styles
- The use of the empty number line for modelling mental calculations
- Children's avoidance of common misconceptions, and the use of activities that directly challenge misconceptions rather than contributing to them
- Teachers' marking that is accurate and efficient and which provides clear and positive feedback about children's learning against the learning objective and ways of progressing

A newly appointed or potential mathematics coordinator can gain a valuable insight into current teaching and obtain a good cross-section of views by talking to a number of people. The coordinator must be open about the issues he or she wants to explore, and not try to gain information in an underhand way. It may be possible to establish:

- Current practices across the school
- Areas where there are problems capable of solution
- Levels of confidence and subject knowledge of staff
- Strengths in the current provision which could be shared and celebrated
- Ideas for change that are already gathering strength in the school
- Reasons for the current standards in performance in testing
- The real issues rather than those perceived by the coordinator at first glance or those raised by purely looking at performance in testing

The coordinator could consider gathering the views of:

- Pupils
- Parents
- Staff
- Support staff and teaching assistants
- Head teacher
- The governor with responsibility for mathematics
- Local secondary schools

In the light of such audits and conversations, the potential coordinator may well identify areas of strengths and areas to be developed and, in consultation with the head teacher, draw up a subject development plan.

For example: the coordinator might establish that there is particularly good use of play in the mathematics lessons of a Year 1 teacher. Children being allowed time, space and resources to play in an unstructured way, while the teacher and teaching assistant observe and assess learning, which then feeds into the planning of more formal mathematics lessons. This strength could be shared and celebrated if other Foundation Stage and Key Stage 1 teachers observed the Year 1 teacher, and if play throughout the school was made the focus of a staff meeting. The coordinator may also find that certain staff lack confidence in the teaching of data handling, and this may be confirmed by a study of the performance in testing throughout Key Stage 2. In addition an audit of ICT and mathematics resources may reveal a shortage of good-quality graphing packages and textbooks that are slightly out of date in this area, representing data in ways that do not reflect the interests and backgrounds of the children in the school. The coordinator could do a number of things to put this right. New software may be purchased, following consultation with the ICT coordinator. The coordinator could evaluate this and then present it to staff in a workshop-type staff meeting where they have chance to try it themselves. The staff could be encouraged to use the software with their classes, and its use could be evaluated in a later staff meeting. The coordinator may also help the staff to make links between the teaching of data handling and other areas of the curriculum that lend themselves to the collecting, representing, and interpreting of data. Termly plans could be annotated with these links and topics reordered when necessary. In addition the timetabling of ICT suites and laptop computers might be adjusted. Where necessary, the coordinator might present a staff meeting on data handling, looking at the types of charts and graphs suitable for each year group and demonstrating the cycle of posing questions, gathering and representing data, and interpreting it to gain answers. In this way effective teaching and learning in data handling could be disseminated throughout the staff. Then the coordinator may identify training courses for members of staff and promote teachers' observation of each other's data-handling lessons.

The effectiveness of the action of the coordinator can be monitored by continuing dialogue with teachers and by studying performance in testing. Sharing of children's work on data handling to make a whole-school display would further demonstrate progression and celebrate success.

Summary

In this chapter we have looked at the desirability of having a member of staff in school or pre-school who can maintain an overview in order to ensure continuity and progression of learning and enhance and support the teaching of mathematics.

Some of the roles typically undertaken by the mathematics subject leader include keeping up to date with current issues and developments in mathematics education, providing support for subject knowledge, helping teachers and practitioners to make cross-curricular connections, managing the mathematics budget, organizing resources, including ICT, and monitoring teaching and learning across the school. The coordinator may also be responsible for monitoring whole-school standards in mathematics and setting targets, as well as providing a written policy for mathematics.

Students in training or newly qualified teachers might draw on the expertise of the coordinator for help with mathematics planning or with the problems in teaching and learning that crop up from time to time.

Finally we have seen how a teacher might move on to take on the role of mathematics coordinator or subject leader by, for example, working alongside the current coordinator, attending a professional development course on subject leadership and reading around the subject.

Reflective Questions

- In what ways do you rely on your teaching colleagues?
- What sort of colleague do you aim to be yourself within the staff team?
- Why is it important for members of staff to have an overview of learning across the school?
- How do you see your career developing? Can you identify your own professional needs and training and learning process that will ensure your continuing development?

REFERENCES AND FURTHER READING:

Bell, D. and Ritchie, R. (1999) *Towards Effective Subject Leadership in the Primary School*, Buckingham: Open University Press.

Brown, T. (2001) *Co-ordinating Mathematics across the Primary School*, London: Routledge Falmer.

DfES (2001) *Teachers' Standards Framework: Helping You Develop* www.standards.dfes.gov.uk/numeracy.

Donaldson, G. (2002) *Successful Mathematical Leadership in the Primary School*, Exeter: Learning Matters.

Index

gifted and talented 243, 267
grouping 108–13, 161–72, 196, 259, 279

home school gap 21–4, 39–40
homework 54, 76, 240–2, 295

ICT 40–2, 59–61, 73–7, 82, 94–7, 110–7,
    126–9
imagery 65–75, 126, 133, 153
inclusion 40, 136, 169, 193
informal mathematics 12, 16
intended learning outcomes 143, 147
interaction 21–3, 55–60, 67, 88, 121, 147,
    149, 151–2
interactive white board 94, 127, 149, 199
investigations 7, 25, 31, 37, 117, 170–1,
    174, 200

Japan 50–1

language 26, 60–3, 68–70, 72, 77, 82–4, 91,
    94–5, 102, 147, 155–6, 175–80, 250
learning
    intentions 140, 149, 153, 159, 161
    objectives 94–5, 108, 139, 145, 147–8,
    203
listening 69, 92, 123, 138–9, 153, 156, 159,
    161

manipulative 81–3
marking 102, 111, 122, 128–31, 138, 139,
    141, 150, 159–61, 193, 203
mathematization 9, 34
misconceptions 47, 58, 70–4, 77–8, 100,
    102, 106, 110, 122–5, 147, 149–51,
    160–1, 186
modelling 8, 41, 43, 50, 55, 62, 69–70, 73,
    84–5, 102, 109–10, 197, 203
monitoring 70, 93, 95, 110, 189, 191–2, 205
motivation 18, 40, 57, 78, 85, 92, 116–7,
    122, 131, 150, 169, 180–1

National Numeracy Strategy 7–8, 62, 109,
    136–8, 166, 169, 195, 201
number
    line 35, 44–5, 63, 97–100, 148, 169,
    177, 189
    rhyme 12, 178
    system 12, 19, 97–9, 189
    track 44, 63, 84, 86, 97–9, 102

observing 90, 150, 156
outside school 4, 12, 14, 15–8, 25–6, 54, 64,
    84, 95, 152, 157

participation 116–20
peer tutoring 112, 151
planning
    long-term 136
    medium-term 137–8, 195
    short-term 138
play 12, 16–7, 19, 21, 24, 25–7, 31–2,
    34–5, 38–9, 42–4, 47, 71, 74, 84–6,
    90–3, 102, 106, 111–2, 114, 124–5,
    137, 140–1, 143–5, 148, 155–6,
    161, 169, 170, 173, 176, 179, 182,
    189, 192, 197, 199, 204–5
plenary 124, 126, 141, 147, 160
policy makers 7, 33
practical mathematics 30
pre-school 4–5, 16, 23, 25, 38–9, 51, 54,
    80–1, 84, 106, 148, 164, 166, 168,
    186–7, 193, 195, 200
prior experience 82, 95
problem-solving 7, 9, 12, 25, 30–5, 39,
    50–1, 75, 83, 86, 91, 94–5, 114, 121,
    158, 201
processes 43, 51, 69–70, 72, 102, 151, 174,
    176
progression and continuity 43, 51, 69–70, 72,
    102, 151, 174, 176, 192